ESSENTIAL

T0041121

ACOUSTIC GUITAR LESSONS

ISBN 0-634-06835-0

STRING LETTER PUBLISHING

EXCLUSIVELY DISTRIBUTED BY

HAL•LEONARD®
CORPORATION
7777 W. BLUEMOUND RD. P.O. BOX 13819 MILWAUKEE, WI 53213

Visit Hal Leonard Online at
www.halleonard.com

In Australia Contact:
Hal Leonard Australia Pty. Ltd.
22 Taunton Drive P.O. Box 5130
Cheltenham East, 3192 Victoria, Australia
Email: **ausadmin@halleonard.com**

contents

cd track listings

Introduction

There has never been a better time to play the guitar! Guitar makers call this the Golden Age of Lutherie for good reason; it's a time where players of all levels can find high-quality guitars in any price range. But this era could just as easily be called the Golden Age of Guitar Instruction. Never before have we had so many high-quality instructional materials and accurate song transcriptions for virtually any style of music.

In *Essential Acoustic Guitar Lessons*, the experienced teachers at *Acoustic Guitar* offer up something for everyone. The Basics section will help you learn the notes on the guitar's fretboard and get started with barre chords and flatpicking. More advanced lessons include styles as diverse as jazz improvisation, Celtic jigs, slack-key guitar, alternate tunings, and more. You'll even learn how to play your guitar like a bass, if the need arises! If one style particularly grabs you, log on to www.stringletter.com, where you'll find a multitude of books delving into specific styles and techniques.

So pick up your guitar, and let's get started!

Andrew DuBrock
Music Editor

Introduction
and Tune-Up

TRACK
1

Need help with the songs in this book? Ask a question in our free, on-line
support forum in the Guitar Talk section of www.acousticguitar.com.

music notation key

The music in this book is written in standard notation and tablature. Here's how to read it.

STANDARD NOTATION

Standard notation is written on a five-line staff. Notes are written in alphabetical order from A to G.

The duration of a note is determined by three things: the note head, stem, and flag. A whole note (𝅝) equals four beats. A half note (𝅗𝅥) is half of that: two beats. A quarter note (♩) equals one beat, an eighth note (♪) equals half of one beat, and a 16th note (♬) is a quarter beat (there are four 16th notes per beat).

The fraction (4/4, 3/4, 6/8, etc.) or 𝄴 character shown at the beginning of a piece of music denotes the time signature. The top number tells you how many beats are in each measure, and the bottom number indicates the rhythmic value of each beat (4 equals a quarter note, 8 equals an eighth note, 16 equals a 16th note, and 2 equals a half note). The most common time signature is 4/4, which signifies four quarter notes per measure and is sometimes designated with the symbol 𝄴 (for common time). The symbol 𝄵 stands for cut time (2/2). Most songs are either in 4/4 or 3/4.

TABLATURE

In tablature, the six horizontal lines represent the six strings of the guitar, with the first string on the top and sixth on the bottom. The numbers refer to fret numbers on a given string. The notation and tablature in this book are designed to be used in tandem—refer to the notation to get the rhythmic information and note durations, and refer to the tablature to get the exact locations of the notes on the guitar fingerboard.

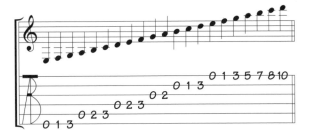

FINGERINGS

Fingerings are indicated with small numbers and letters in the notation. Left-hand (fretting-hand) fingering is indicated with 1 for the index finger, 2 the middle, 3 the ring, 4 the pinky, and *T* the thumb. Right-hand fingering is indicated by *i* for the index finger, *m* the middle, *a* the ring, *c* the pinky, and *p* the thumb. Remember that the fingerings indicated are only suggestions; if you find a different way that works better for you, use it.

CHORD DIAGRAMS

Chord diagrams show where the fingers go on the fingerboard. Frets are shown horizontally. The thick top line represents the nut. A Roman numeral to the right of a diagram indicates a chord played higher up the neck (in this case the top horizontal line is thin). Strings are shown as vertical lines. The line on the far left represents the sixth (lowest) string, and the line on the far right represents the first (highest) string. Dots show where the fingers go, and thick horizontal lines indicate barres. Numbers above the diagram are left-hand finger numbers, as used in standard notation. Again, the fingerings are only suggestions. An *X* indicates a string that should be muted or not played; 0 indicates an open string.

CAPOS

If a capo is used, a Roman numeral indicates the fret where the capo should be placed. The standard notation and tablature is written as if the capo were the nut of the guitar. For instance, a tune capoed anywhere up the neck and played using key-of-G chord shapes and fingerings will be written in the key of G. Likewise, open strings held down by the capo are written as open strings.

TUNINGS

Alternate guitar tunings are given from the lowest (sixth) string to the highest (first) string. For instance, D A D G B E indicates standard tuning with the bottom string dropped to D. Standard notation for songs in alternate tunings always reflects the actual pitches of the notes.

VOCAL TUNES

Vocal tunes are sometimes written with a fully tabbed-out introduction and a vocal melody with chord diagrams for the rest of the piece. The tab intro is usually your indication of which strum or fingerpicking pattern to use in the rest of the piece. The melody with lyrics underneath is the melody sung by the vocalist. Occasionally smaller notes are written with the melody to indicate the harmony part sung by another vocalist. These are not to be confused with cue notes, which are small notes that indicate melodies that vary when a section is repeated. Listen to a recording of the piece to get a feel for the guitar accompaniment and to hear the singing if you aren't skilled at reading vocal melodies.

ARTICULATIONS

There are a number of ways you can articulate a note on the guitar. Notes connected with slurs (not to be confused with ties) in the tablature or standard notation are articulated with either a hammer-on, pull-off, or slide. Lower notes slurred to higher notes are played as hammer-ons; higher notes slurred to lower notes are played as pull-offs. While it's usually obvious that slurred notes are played as hammer-ons or pull-offs, an *H* or *P* is included above the tablature as an extra reminder.

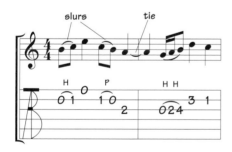

Slides are represented with a dash, and an *S* is included above the tab. A dash preceding a note represents a slide into the note from an indefinite point in the direction of the slide; a dash following a note indicates a slide off of the note to an indefinite point in the direction of the slide. For two slurred notes connected with a slide, you should pick the first note and then slide into the second.

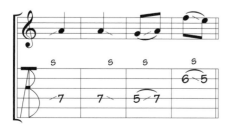

Bends are represented with upward curves, as shown in the next example. Most bends have a specific destination pitch—

the number above the bend symbol shows how much the bend raises the string's pitch: ¼ for a slight bend, ½ for a half step, 1 for a whole step.

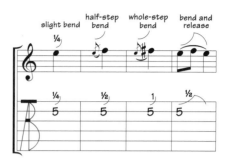

HARMONICS

Harmonics are represented by diamond-shaped notes in the standard notation and a small dot next to the tablature numbers. Natural harmonics are indicated with the text "Harmonics" or "Harm." above the tablature. Harmonics articulated with the right hand (often called artificial harmonics) include the text "R.H. Harmonics" or "R.H. Harm." above the tab. Right-hand harmonics are executed by lightly touching the harmonic node (usually 12 frets above the open string or fretted note) with the right-hand index finger and plucking the string with the thumb or ring finger or pick. For extended phrases played with right-hand harmonics, the fretted notes are shown in the tab along with instructions to touch the harmonics 12 frets above the notes.

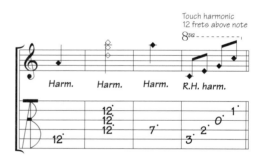

REPEATS

One of the most confusing parts of a musical score can be the navigation symbols, such as repeats, *D.S. al Coda, D.C. al Fine, To Coda,* etc.

Repeat symbols are placed at the beginning and end of the passage to be repeated.

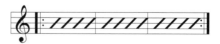

You should ignore repeat symbols with the dots on the right side the first time you encounter them; when you come to a repeat symbol with dots on the left side, jump back to the previous repeat symbol facing the opposite direction (if there is no previous symbol, go to the beginning of the piece). The next time you come to the repeat symbol, ignore it and keep going unless it includes instructions such as "Repeat three times."

A section will often have a different ending after each repeat. The example below includes a first and a second ending. Play until you hit the repeat symbol, jump back to the previous repeat symbol and play until you reach the bracketed first ending, skip the measures under the bracket and jump immediately to the second ending, and then continue.

of the piece when you encounter this indication. Both *D.C.* and *D.S.* are usually accompanied by *al Fine* or *al Coda*. *Fine* indicates the end of a piece. A coda is a final passage near the end of a piece and is indicated with ⊕. *D.S. al Coda* simply tells you to jump back to the sign and continue on until you are instructed to jump to the coda, indicated with *To Coda* ⊕.

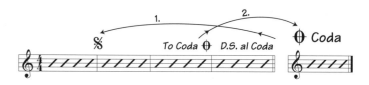

D.S. stands for *dal segno* or "from the sign." When you encounter this indication, jump immediately to the sign (𝄋). *D.C.* stands for *da capo* or "from the beginning." Jump to the top

D.C. al Fine tells you to jump to the beginning of a tune and continue until you encounter the *Fine* indicating the end of the piece (ignore the *Fine* the first time through).

about the teachers

KEOLA BEAMER

Keola Beamer is a master slack-key guitarist who compiled the first comprehensive teaching manual on slack-key, *Hawaiian Slack Key Guitar* (Oak Publications), and helped spark a statewide revival of the tradition. He has received numerous *Nä Hökü* Hanohano Awards (the Hawaiian Grammy) for his contributions to the art form, and in 1998 he released the instructional video *The Art of Hawaiian Slack Key Guitar* (Homespun Tapes). His latest critically acclaimed solo recording is *Ka LeoO Loko—Soliloquy*, released on Dancing Cat Records. For more information, visit www.kbeamer.com.

ANDREW DuBROCK

Andrew DuBrock grew up playing piano and horn and singing in choir. While pursuing a degree in music at Brown University, he decided it was finally time to pick up the guitar. In 1994, he began editing Hal Leonard's Signature Licks, Musicians' Institute, and Guitar School series. He also penned Acoustic Café, a monthly column in Cherry Lane's *Guitar One* magazine. He now translates outlandish tunings and bizarre techniques to paper as *Acoustic Guitar's* music editor, and performs around the San Francisco area as a singer-songwriter and with his band DuBROCK (www.dubrock.net).

JAMIE FINDLAY

Jamie Findlay, a master of contemporary acoustic jazz guitar, is on the faculty of the Musicians Institute in Hollywood, California. Findlay is a busy performer and composer, with two CDs under his own name, *Wings of Light Amigos del Corazón* (Acoustic Music Records), and others with the Acoustic Jazz Quartet, Duck Baker, and more. He has released three videos and five books and is currently working on an original solo CD as well as an instructional book/CD, *Miles Davis for Solo Guitar* (Hal Leonard). Check out Findlay's Web site at www.jamiefindlay.com.

CHRIS GRAMPP

Chris Grampp has been playing a wide range of guitar styles, including jazz, swing, blues, and rock, for 35 years. He studied with Tuck Andress, Howard Roberts, and George Barnes and leads his own eclectic band, Club Sandwich. Grampp has taught at the California Coast Music Camp, the Puget Sound Guitar Workshop, and the Sound Acoustic Music Camp and has led workshops at numerous festivals, including the Strawberry Music Festival and the Sonoma County Folk Festival.

DAVID HAMBURGER

David Hamburger is a performer and writer who lives in Austin, Texas. He has been playing folk and blues music since first picking up the guitar at the age of 12 and has been on the faculty of the National Guitar Workshop since 1988. Hamburger's guitar, slide guitar, and Dobro playing can be heard on his solo albums *King of the Brooklyn Delta* (Chester, 1994) and *Indigo Rose* (Chester, 1999), as well as on numerous other independent recordings. Hamburger is the author of many books, including *The Acoustic Guitar Method*, and has contributed dozens of lessons and articles to *Guitar Player* and *Acoustic Guitar* magazines. For a discography, performance schedule, and other information, visit his website at www.davidhamburger.com.

KAREN HOGG

Karen Hogg is a multi-instrumentalist, music teacher, yoga teacher, and freelance writer living in New York City. She has written two instructional books for Workshop Arts/Alfred Publishing: *Women in Rock* and *Guitar Made Easy*. Hogg has been teaching for ten years and is an instructor at the National Guitar Summer Workshop and the American Institute of Guitar. She performs regularly on guitar and mandolin in various country and rock bands around New York.

PAUL KOTAPISH

Paul Kotapish started playing guitar in bands shortly after he first heard the Beatles on his transistor radio. He has toured the globe and recorded numerous albums with Irish fiddler Kevin Burke, the Hillbillies from Mars, and Wake the Dead (www.wakethedead.org), an acoustic ensemble that meshes Grateful Dead songs with traditional Irish music. During the day he messes around on computers doing forensic multimedia work for an Oakland, California law firm.

TONY MARCUS

Tony Marcus plays lead guitar and violin in the '30s and '40s swing band Cats and Jammers, which records for the Tuxedo label (2557 Wakefield Ave., Oakland, CA 94606). He's also played with the Arkansas Sheiks, the Cheap Suit Serenaders (featuring counter-culture cartoonist Robert Crumb), and the Royal Society Jazz Orchestra.

PETER MULVEY

Peter Mulvey began his musical career playing guitar in the subways of Boston and on the streets of Dublin. Since those early busking days, he has recorded four critically acclaimed albums (his latest, *Ten Thosand Mornings*, was released in 2002) and has captivated audiences across the U.S. and Ireland with his intelligent lyrics and percussive, inventive guitar work. You can find him on the Web at www.petermulvey.com.

SCOTT NYGAARD

Scott Nygaard is an accomplished guitarist with more than 30 years of teaching, performing, and recording experience. He lives in San Francisco, California, and is the editor of Acoustic Guitar magazine, whose staff he joined in 1997. He has performed and recorded with such artists as Chris Thile, Tim O'Brien, Laurie Lewis, and Jerry Douglas; released two albums, No Hurry and Dreamer's Waltz, on Rounder Records; and been nominated for a number of Grammies for his work on other artists' CDs. He currently performs with Darol Anger's American Fiddle Ensemble and singers Chris and Cassie Webster. Both groups released CDs in early 2004.

MARK SMALL

Classical guitarist/composer Mark Small is a performer and widely published music journalist who lives in Foxboro, Massachusetts. Small is editor of *Berklee Today* magazine. He has released six CDs with the Mark Small/Robert Torres Guitar Duo. Their latest is *Winterlight II: Gabriel's Message* (Shadow Mountain). Mel Bay has published a three-volume series of graded guitar duets transcribed and edited by Small and Torres. For information and sound and video clips, visit www.smalltorresduo.com.

DAVID SURETTE

David Surette is a guitar and mandolin player from South Berwick, Maine. He performs regularly in a duo with singer Susie Burke or fiddler Rodney Miller, as a solo fingerstyle guitarist, and as a freelance accompanist. He has released several recordings, including *Sometimes in the Evening* with Susie Burke and *New Leaf* with Rodney Miller. Surette is an experienced teacher and is the folk coordinator at the Concord Community Music School in Concord, New Hampshire. He has recently worked on a book for Mel Bay Publications called *Northern Roots: New England, French-Canadian, and Irish Dance Music for Guitar.*

HAPPY TRAUM

During the past 40 years, Happy Traum's avid interest in traditional and contemporary music has brought him recognition as a performer, writer, editor, folklorist, teacher, and recording artist. He has performed throughout the world and has appeared on recordings as a featured artist, as well as on sessions with Bob Dylan, Chris Smither, Maria Muldaur, Eric Andersen, Rory Block, Jerry Jeff Walker, Allen Ginsberg, and many others. Traum is the author of more than a dozen bestselling guitar instruction books and, as founder of Homespun Tapes, has produced more than 400 music lessons taught by top professional performing musicians on videos, CDs, and cassettes.

Unlocking the Fretboard
Karen Hogg

Notes on the Fretboard

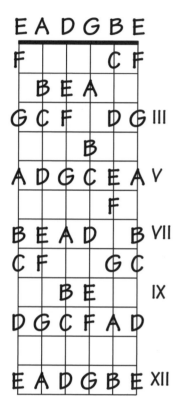

When you first start playing the guitar, just moving around and getting from one chord to the next can be a challenge. Many of us memorize fingerings and patterns for scales and chords to make this process easier. This is a viable way of learning that achieves an important goal—it gets you playing right away. However, many people memorize patterns on the guitar without really knowing what they are playing. Fretboard knowledge—knowing where each note is located on your guitar—can help you break free of the same old scale patterns and chord fingerings. In addition, understanding the fretboard can help you get more out of the patterns you already know. In this lesson, we will learn to map out all the natural notes (the notes of the C-major scale) on the guitar.

Naming the open strings is the first step. From high to low, they are: E (first string), B (second string), G (third string), D (fourth string), A (fifth string), and E (sixth string). Take a look at the diagram on this page.

When mapping out the fretboard, it is useful to know that there are certain intervals, or spaces, between each of the notes. A half step, or minor second, is the distance from one fret to the next. The space between the first fret of any string and the second fret on that same string is a half step. A whole step, or a major second, is the distance between two frets. The space between the first fret of any string and the third fret of that same string is a whole step. Example 1 shows the intervals between each of the natural notes.

Example 2 shows notes on the first string, E. The open string is an E note. Since the notes go up in alphabetical order, the next note is F, a half step up on the first fret. G, the following note, is a whole step up from F on the third fret. A is located on the fifth fret, a whole step up from G. Next is B, a whole step up on the seventh fret. C is found on the eighth fret, a half step up. D is on the tenth fret, a whole step away from C. Next is E, a whole step up on the 12th fret. The octave of each open string is at the 12th fret (a good thing to know when learning your fretboard).

Ex. 1

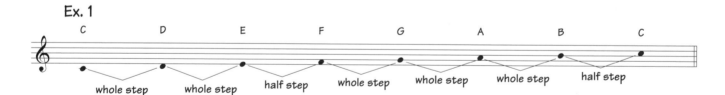

As you're finding these notes, play them and sing the name of the note aloud. This will reinforce them in your memory. Play the notes going up and down the neck.

TRACK 2
Ex. 2
Notes on the high E string

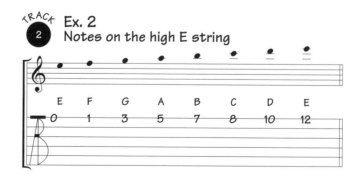

Example 3 illustrates the notes on the second string, B. Example 4 shows the notes going up the third string, G. And Examples 5–7 map out the notes of the fourth (D), fifth (A), and sixth (E) strings. Play each note and say or sing the letter names aloud as you play them.

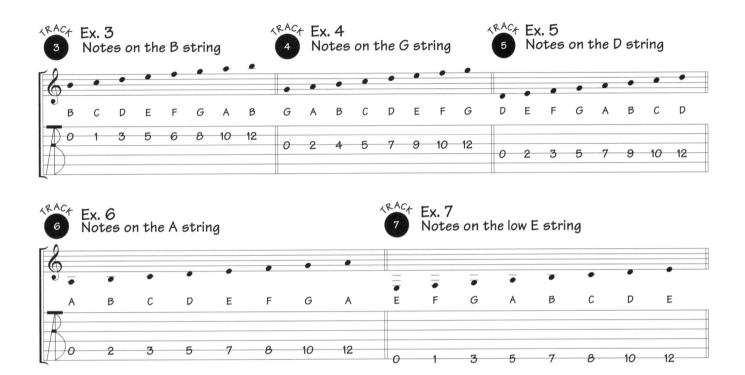

After practicing Examples 1–7 backward and forward while singing or naming the notes, there are several other things you can do to learn the fretboard. One is to memorize the notes across a particular fret. Example 8 shows the notes on the fifth fret on every string. This memorized fret can act as a road marker on your fretboard. If you know the fifth fret on your sixth string is an A note, then the seventh fret, a whole step above, must be a B note. If the fifth fret on the second string is an E note, then the sixth fret, a half step above, must be an F note, etc.

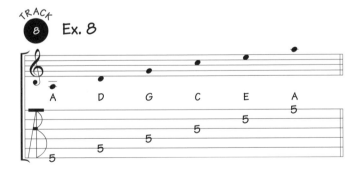

Another useful exercise is to pick a note at random and try to find it at least once on each string. For instance, try to find C on every string, as shown in Example 9. This exercise is time consuming at first, but it will further enhance your familiarity with the guitar's fingerboard.

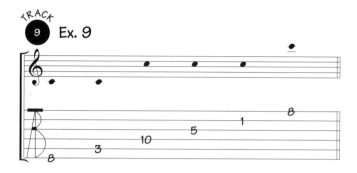

The next step, after learning where single notes are located, is to find out where groups of notes are located in relation to each other. One way of doing this is to map out a familiar melody in a couple different areas of the guitar neck. Example 10 shows "Twinkle, Twinkle Little Star" played in open position. In Example 11, the same melody is played starting on the fifth fret of the fourth string without using open strings. Example 12 shows the tune starting on the tenth fret of the fifth string. You can also try this with your own songs. Take a chord progression or a melody line you've been working on and find at least three different ways to play it on the guitar.

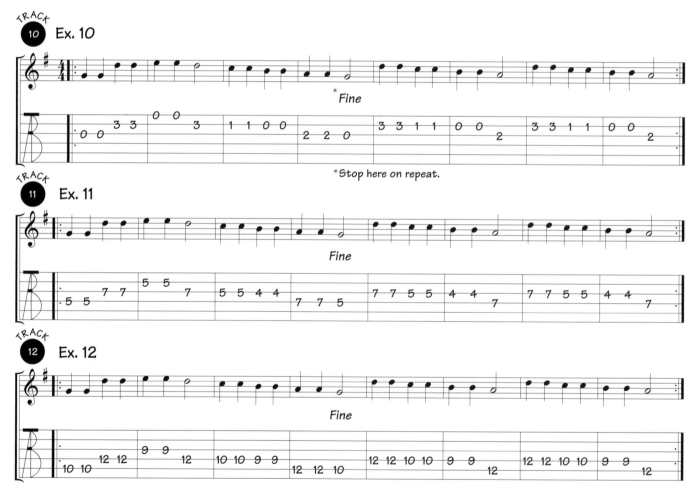

It is important to remember that you will not learn your fretboard overnight. Be patient with yourself and be consistent in your practice. Even if you dedicate just five minutes of each practice session to building your fretboard knowledge, you will reap the benefits. Transposing to different keys and finding new chord voicings and melodies will be much easier, because now you'll know where the notes within these scales and chords are located!

Barre Chords

David Hamburger

Once you've gotten comfortable with the basic open-position chords—G, C, D, A, or any other chord with at least one or two open strings in it—you may be tempted to branch out into *barre chords*. Playing a barre chord involves holding down most or all of the strings across a single fret (i.e., in a "barre" across the fingerboard) and using some combination of your remaining three fretting fingers to form the rest of the chord. With no open strings, barre chords sound really different from open chords, and they are part of the family of *movable chord forms,* or shapes that can be moved up and down the neck.

TWO BASIC SHAPES

Barre chords really only come in two basic shapes. If you've ever played an open-E chord or an open-A chord using a capo, you'll be able to see what these two shapes are. Take a look at them:

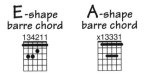

The first one is like a capoed E chord, only your index finger is acting as the capo. The second one is like a capoed A chord with your index finger acting as the capo. Try holding these chords with your index-finger barre at the third fret. One difference with the A-shape chord is that you can't really get the high string to sound at the third fret unless your ring finger is double-jointed. You don't want to hear the high string fretted at the fifth fret, so try raising your ring finger at that point just enough to mute the high string, which most people's hands are just flexible enough to allow.

E-SHAPE BARRE

When you first learn a new open chord, you often need to put your fingers down one by one, forming the shape as a collection of individual locations on the fretboard. Obviously, you don't have time to do that during a song, so the essential transition between learning and using a chord involves teaching your hand to land on that set of frets and strings as a group. It's the same with barre chords.

Here's one exercise to help you learn to move your fingers as a group. Start by forming the following G chord:

With the chord in place, lift all your fingers together and hold them, hovering, over the fretboard. Try and hold them together as if you were playing the chord in the air. Now drop them down onto the strings, and see how close they are to where they should be. Take a little time to adjust them and get them all on the right frets and strings, and then do the whole thing again. Over time, you'll find yourself landing more accurately on the chord you want.

The next step is to start trying to play chord progressions. The cool thing about barre chords is that they're movable shapes: with no open strings, you can just move one shape around to get all kinds of chords. "Aha," I hear you say, "and just how do I know what chord I'm playing if they all look the same?"

Good point. The clue is to go back to our idea that this is like playing an open chord over a capo, where your finger is the capo itself. Since this first shape is like capoing an E chord, and the root of an E chord is on the sixth string, any barre chord you play using this shape will take its name from whatever note your index finger is covering on the sixth string. That's why this chord shape is also called a *sixth-string root voicing.*

If you play this shape at the third fret, you get a G chord, because the root note of the chord shape (the sixth string) is on a G. Move up a whole step to the fifth fret and now your index finger is on A, so you've got an A chord. Here's a table of some of the main chords you can get going up the neck:

Fret	Chord
I	F
III	G
V	A
VII	B
VIII	C
X	D

Now we know enough to do something important, something with serious historic and cultural significance: playing the chords to "Wild Thing." Example 1 shows the chords to "Wild Thing" in the key of G. The chords are G, C, and D, so we'll play our barre chord shape at the third, eighth, and tenth frets.

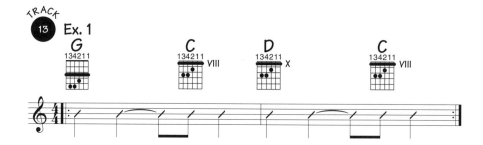

Now, that just wouldn't sound the same with open chords, would it?

As you move from chord to chord, you don't even really have to lift your fingers—just relax them enough to slide up and down the strings and press them back into place when you get where you're going. Yeah, the strings are going to squeak. When you get up to speed, you won't really notice it as much.

Perhaps not all your notes are ringing out clearly. In fact, if these are your first barre chords ever, they're probably not. That's OK. If you really want the sound of strings ringing and sustaining, you should probably play open chords with or without a capo or use a solid-body electric guitar with skinny strings and a big ol' amplifier. Barre chords are most useful when you want to play tight, staccato-sounding things and maintain more control over your guitar's sustain than you can with open strings.

A-SHAPE BARRE

Let's check out the other shape, the one we'll call the *A-shape* because it's like capoing an A chord, with your index finger taking the place of the capo. This shape is sort of a double whammy, because in addition to barring with your index finger, you're also barring the rest of the required notes with your ring finger at the same time. But there is some good news: you're only covering five strings with your index finger instead of six, and the only one that really has to ring clear is the fifth string itself. Also, the high string is supposed to be muted by the underside of your ring finger, which is probably happening without your even trying. If the high string is ringing out, giving you that end-of-a-Beatles-song sound (a major-sixth chord), just let up the pressure a little with your ring finger at the high string and you should be able to mute it. Finally, if you're not doing so already, try putting your thumb along the back of the neck for more leverage.

Try the same exercise we did with the E-shape barre chord to teach your fingers this chord shape: form the chord on the strings, lift your fingers off as a group, hold them in the air over the fingerboard, and try to drop them into place all together onto the right strings/frets.

If we tried to play the "Wild Thing" chord progression in C using the E-shape barre chord, we'd run out of neck, at least on a standard, noncutaway acoustic guitar. The A-shape barre chord has its root on the fifth string, so if you can name a few notes on the fifth string, you can find your way around. Example 2 shows how you can play this progression in C by starting at the third fret for C, going up to the eighth fret for F, and the tenth fret for G.

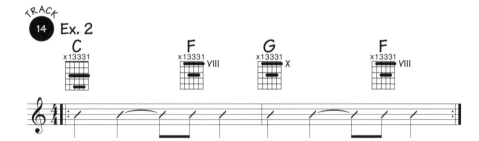

Here's a table of where you can find some of those "most wanted" chords, which can be referred to as fifth-string root voicings:

Fret	Chord
I	B♭
II	B
III	C
V	D
VII	E
VIII	F
X	G

COMBINING THE SHAPES

So far we've worked with two different chord shapes, one with its root on the sixth string and one with its root on the fifth string. By using these two shapes together we can begin to play chord progressions in a much more compact way on the neck.

Keep imagining these chords as capoed versions of open chords for a minute. Suppose you started with a I–IV–V chord progression in E and then capoed it at the third fret. You'd play an E shape for the I, which would now sound like a G chord, and you'd play an A shape for the IV, and that would sound like a C chord. Everything would be close together; you wouldn't have to jump around at all to get from the "E" (which is sounding like a G) to the "A" (which is sounding like a C).

We can do the same kind of thing with barre chords. Start with a G barre chord at the third fret, and move over to a C barre chord, also at the third fret. Move that C chord up two frets, and you've got a D—the V chord in the key of G. So we can play our fave I–IV–V tune with these chords, as in Example 3.

Now we're hardly moving around the neck at all. And, if we want this same song up a whole step, we can just start at the fifth fret instead of the third fret, as in Example 4. Voilà—we've just transposed the song from G to A.

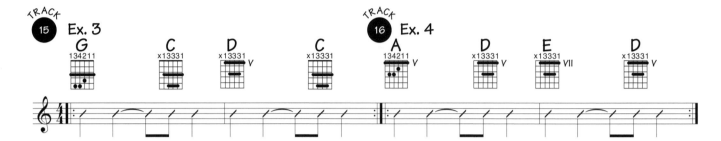

Now suppose that you were capoed up at the tenth fret. If you played an open A-shape chord, it would sound like a G chord. When you play an A in open position, where's the V? It's the E chord. So if you started at the tenth fret using the A-shape barre chord for the I, or G, then your V—that is, your D chord—would also be at the tenth fret, using the E-shape barre chord. You couldn't move that D chord down two frets, to the eighth fret, if you had a capo on at the tenth fret, but you can do it with barre chords by just moving your hand. Move your D chord down two frets and you've got a C chord, or the IV chord. Example 5 runs through the "Wild Thing" chords at this position. Again, we only have to move two frets, maximum, to get the whole chord progression.

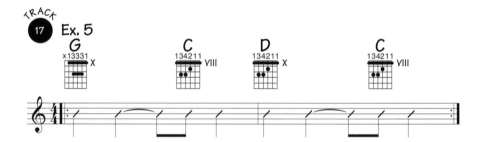

POWER CHORDS

Here's an idea straight out of electric rock guitar: the power chord. Power chords are just the bottom two notes of a barre chord—the root and fifth of the chord. Electric guitarists use them because all those extra tones on the upper strings clutter things up and clash with each other when you pour them through a loud, distorted amp. Plus, they're a lot easier to play, especially when your guitar is hanging somewhere around your knees. Example 6 runs through the "Wild Thing" progression with power chords. Grab the bottom note of each chord with your index finger and the upper note with your ring finger, play a bunch of downstrokes while partially muting the strings with your palm, and rock on.

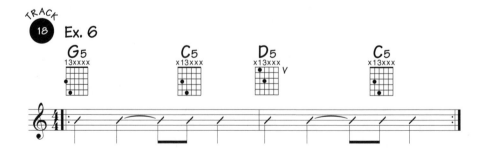

Flatpicking 101

David Hamburger

When you're learning to play single notes with a pick, it's good to develop a solid sense of time. Moving a single-note melody forward with fire and conviction is as much about solid timing as it is about hitting the right notes and creating a great tone. If you primarily play slow melodies full of quarter notes and half notes, how you pick each note won't matter as much, but when you try stringing long sequences of eighth and 16th notes together, it's important to learn to play with alternating down- and upstrokes if you want to get the right rhythmic feel.

That feel comes from your right hand, just like it does for rhythm guitar parts. The key is to zero in on how and when you play downstrokes and upstrokes—that is, when you should pick down on a string, with your pick heading toward the ground, and when you should pick up on a string, with the pick headed back toward your face. The idea is to train your hand to play downstrokes on the onbeats. In a measure of 4/4 (four beats to a measure), you should play downstrokes on beats 1, 2, 3, and 4, as shown in Example 1.

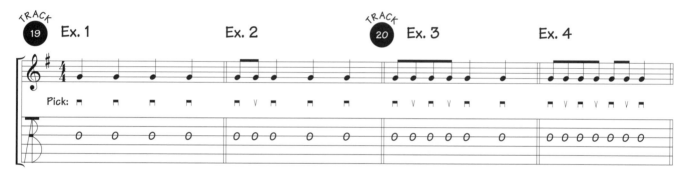

Next, you want to train your hand to play upstrokes on the upbeats—the notes that fall on the *and* of each beat. In Example 2, add one upstroke on the *and* of beat 1. Now add an upstroke on the *and* of beat 2, as in Example 3. In Example 4, you've got upstrokes on the *ands* of beats 1, 2, and 3. Finally, in Example 5, you've got an upstroke on the *and* of all four beats. What you're shooting for is shown in Example 5: a steady alternation of downstrokes and upstrokes. Try playing through a piece of the G-major scale, picking each note twice, with an upstroke and a downstroke, as in Example 6.

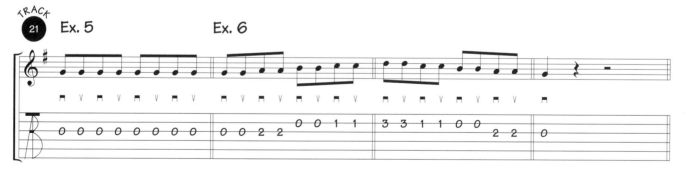

You may notice that it takes a little practice to keep things moving smoothly when you change strings. Things get even more complicated once you start crossing strings more frequently and at less predictable moments in a scale or melody. Examples 7–10 are four exercises that will help you maintain consistent down and up picking while playing more than one string. In Example 7, you reach up for a downstroke on the second string just after an upstroke on the third string. In Example 8, you play two notes in a row on the G string followed by a note on the D string, requiring you to make the opposite jump, from a downstroke on the third string to an upstroke on the fourth string. In Examples 9 and 10, make sure you maintain consistent down- and upstrokes as you play across three strings.

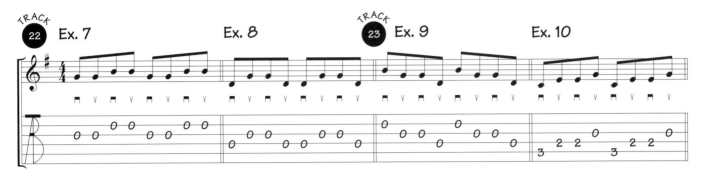

Now, let's take these new moves out for a spin on the first half, or *A section*, of the fiddle tune "Blackberry Blossom," which is found at the end of the lesson. The A section is the first eight measures of the tune. Notice the spots where you need to *backpick*, or jump from a downstroke on one string to an upstroke on the string below. This happens in several places, including beat 4 of measure 1, beats 2 and 3 of measure 2, beat 2 of measure 3, and in similar places in the melody in measures 5 and 6. A little extra time with Examples 8 and 9 can help make moments like these easier to work out.

You'll find that if you practice this often and really concentrate on keeping your down- and upstrokes in the right place, you will reach the point where you can just wind up like a typewriter and go, as long as you've got nothing but steady eighth notes. The key is to be able to leave notes out and still play each onbeat with a downstroke and each *and* with an upstroke.

Check out Example 11, which omits every other upbeat. Make sure you come in on beat 3 with a downstroke. Next we'll try leaving out a downstroke. Try Example 12, and pay close attention to where the upstrokes land.

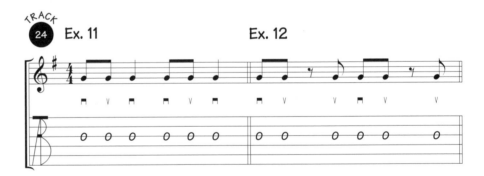

One thing that can really help is to try and keep your picking hand moving during the rest—the note you're not playing. Move your hand as if you were picking another downstroke, but keep your pick out in front of the strings so you get no sound. It's like you're pretending to play the downstroke. Your hand will look like it's still playing solid eighth notes—straight up-and-down picking—and more importantly, it will feel that way.

Next, let's try a couple of examples of how this kind of picking might crop up in an actual tune. Examples 13 and 14 are from the second part of "Blackberry Blossom." Example 13 begins with a big string skip, from the fourth to the first string. Example 14 omits the second and fourth downbeats while changing notes on the same string.

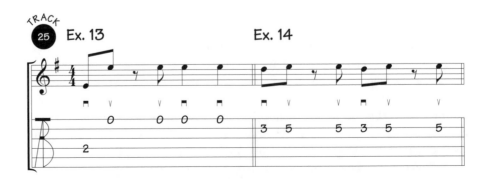

To wrap things up, let's tackle the entire second half, or *B section*, of "Blackberry Blossom" (bars 9–16). Keep your picking hand moving through those imaginary downstrokes on beat 2 of measures 10, 12, and 14. In measures 9, 11, and 13, make sure every quarter note gets played with a downstroke, and notice how you play the high string with a downstroke on beat 2, followed by an upstroke on the second string.

When you've got both the A and B sections down, you can put it all together by playing the A section twice, followed by the B section twice. This is the usual form of the tune and is often abbreviated AABB.

Working through an actual tune like this is a good way to concentrate on that rhythmic drive your right hand needs without feeling, in the words of one student of mine, "like you're wasting your life on boring technique exercises." Just remember to play your downbeats with downstrokes, and soon you'll have the best time of anyone in your neighborhood. Good luck!

Blackberry Blossom

Traditional, arranged by David Hamburger

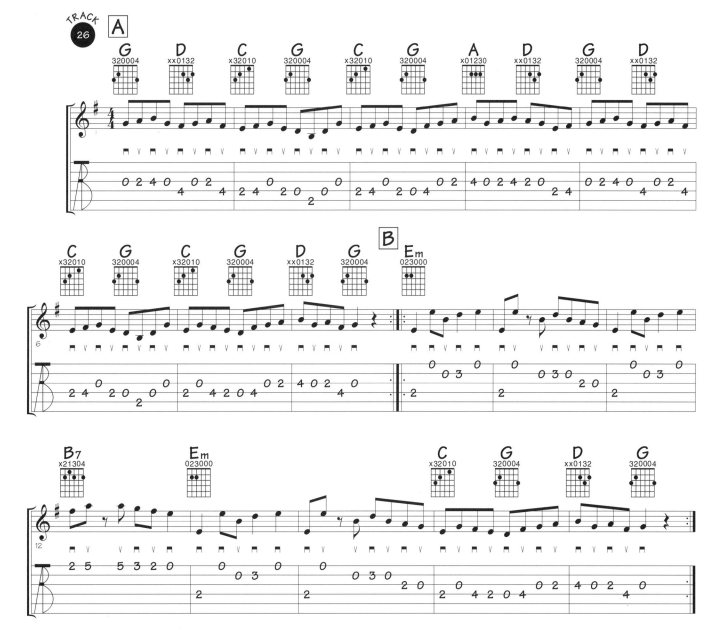

Bluegrass in Dropped D
Happy Traum

Dropped D is my favorite tuning. I use it for the majority of my arrangements, especially those in which the song is in the key of D, G, or D minor. In these keys, the low D can be used to best advantage. The lowered sixth string provides a wonderfully rich bass sound, and it allows me to play in different positions on the fingerboard more easily than when the string is tuned to the standard E.

The key of D is most commonly associated with this tuning, with its emphasis on the root note of the tonic (D) chord. However, I also like to use dropped-D tuning for songs in G, because the dominant chord in G (D7) gives me a chance to use the low D in a different place in the song. It also gives me a nice alternate bass note when I am strumming the G chord, so instead of going from G to the D on the open fourth string, I can use the D on the open sixth string.

If you haven't played in dropped D before, don't be intimidated by the idea of changing your guitar tuning. It's really quite easy, and with practice it can be done with a mere twist of the wrist. All you have to do is loosen your sixth string until the sound is one whole tone lower, from E to D. It will now be one octave below your open fourth string, which will help you get it in tune. You can also check to see if the low D is in tune by fretting the sixth string at the seventh fret and matching it against your open fifth string (A). Of course, an electronic tuner would be a big help too.

Because this string is now tuned to a different note, you'll have to adjust some of your chord positions. The G chord is a little more of a stretch because the root note (G) is now at the fifth fret instead of the third. Since you can no longer reach the B note on the second fret of the fifth string, you'll have to avoid playing the open fifth string. I usually just damp it by letting my ring finger touch it slightly. You can also use your little finger to play the fifth fret of the fifth string, which doubles the D note of the open fourth string. It won't be hard once you get used to it.

When changing to the G from another chord, I often find myself sliding up to the G note in the bass with my ring finger, starting a couple of frets below it. This gives me a little more time to get my hand into position. It also adds a nice, ear-catching sound to that first bass note of the new chord. You can also add emphasis to the C chord by adding a slide or hammer-on to the bass C note (see measure 11 of "Angel Band").

Another chord that's a little tricky is the G7, which is most easily played in dropped-D tuning by using the F note at the third fret of the fourth string as the bass note (see diagram below). To play an E-minor chord, which is often used in the key of G, you just have to raise the normally open sixth string to E by fretting it at the second fret. And when you play a C chord, you'll have to avoid the sixth string, but the sound of the low D on the D or D7 chords will make up for this.

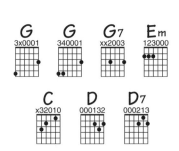

"Angel Band" is an easy but beautiful old bluegrass gospel song that works very well in this tuning. It's in 3/4 (waltz) time, and the rhythm backup technique I use is often referred to as Carter Family style. A bass note is followed by two down-up strums on the top two or three strings. This is counted as *one, two*-and, *three*-and, *one, two*-and, *three*-and, etc. You can play it with a pick or your fingers. I like to use my fingers, playing the bass notes with my thumb and the chords with my index and middle fingers, brushing down and up across the top strings. Try to play the bass notes clearly and evenly and a little louder than the chord strums.

I've filled out the basic strum pattern with some bass runs, which "walk" you from one chord to the next by substituting a series of bass notes for the strum. In measures 16 and 20 these notes move down the scale from the root of the G chord to the root of the D chord. In measure 31 the bass run is used to get you to the note that makes the G chord a G7 (F♮), so the run goes up the scale: D, E, F.

I've also added a typical bluegrass lick (measures 7 and 39) to dress up the tune a little. Traditionally known as the G or Flatt run (after the legendary bluegrass singer and guitarist Lester Flatt), this lick has been used by innumerable flatpickers to punctuate a musical line and add excitement to the arrangement. I have written just one of the many ways this lick can be played. The important thing is to get the timing right. The G note that starts the run is on the first beat, and the first chordal strum comes in on the second beat, followed by the two hammer-ons. Count it like this: *one, two* and, *three* and-a, *one*. The final one lands on the G (open third string), followed by the rhythm chords. If you find this too hard to play right now, just keep playing the bass-strum pattern throughout.

The Stanley Brothers, whose superb version of this classic appears on the soundtrack of the hit film *O Brother, Where Art Thou?*, originally recorded it back in the 1950s. This particular version comes from my Homespun instructional video *Fingerstyle Arrangements for Hymns, Spirituals, and Sacred Songs*. I hope you like it.

Angel Band

Traditional, arranged by Happy Traum

1. MY LATEST SUN IS SINKING FAST
   MY RACE IS NEARLY RUN
   MY LONGEST TRIAL NOW IS PAST
   MY TRIUMPH HAS BEGUN

   OH COME ANGEL BAND
   COME AND AROUND ME STAND
   BEAR ME AWAY ON YOUR SNOW-WHITE WINGS
   TO MY IMMORTAL HOME
   BEAR ME AWAY ON YOUR SNOW-WHITE WINGS
   TO MY IMMORTAL HOME

2. I KNOW I'M NEAR THE HOLY RANKS
   OF FRIENDS AND KINDRED DEAR
   I BRUSH THE DEW ON JORDAN'S BANKS
   THE CROSSING MUST BE NEAR

   CHORUS

3. I'VE ALMOST GAINED MY HEAVENLY HOME
   MY SPIRIT LOUDLY SINGS
   THE HOLY ONES, BEHOLD THEY COME
   I HEAR THE NOISE OF WINGS

   CHORUS

4. OH BEAR MY LONGING HEART TO HIM
   WHO BLED AND DIED FOR ME
   WHOSE BLOOD NOW CLEANSES FROM ALL SIN
   AND GIVES ME VICTORY

   CHORUS

Bass Lines for Guitarists

Paul Kotapish

I f you find yourself lost in the thrum at jam sessions or competing for sonic elbow room in your guitar band, consider shifting to the lower strings as a way to carve out your own niche. The treble end of the guitar tends to get most of the hot press, but playing bass is more fun than a box of aardvarks, and it can be every bit as challenging—and satisfying—as spinning out flash lines on the high strings. And while you might be lucky enough to have an electric or acoustic bass at hand, a standard six-string can do a mighty job of driving the bottom end. You might need to learn some new musical vocabulary and a few different techniques, but if you've got even a rudimentary knowledge of the fingerboard, you should be off and thumping like Paul McCartney, Sting, or Derek Smalls in no time.

One of the best ways to make the bottom end of a guitar sound deeper and fatter is to combine low notes with notes an octave higher. The diagrams below show the finger positions for playing octave pairs.

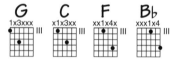

In each example, play the low string with your index finger and the higher note with your ring finger or pinky. When your index finger is on the E or A strings, the octave will be two strings and two frets higher. When you jump to the D and G strings, you'll need to stretch your pinky one fret farther. The secret here is to damp the intervening string with the pad of your index finger and hit the two fretted notes with one quick pluck of pick or fingers, so they sound at the same time.

Try these forms on the extended G scale in Example 1. Eschew open strings and play everything as fretted notes. Notice that your hand position shifts in the second measure as you move across the fretboard. Practice this example until you can easily make the string shifts and each octave pair has a clear sound. Press down just long enough to get a clean attack on both notes, and then quickly release your grip as you move to the next octave.

TRACK 29 Ex. 1

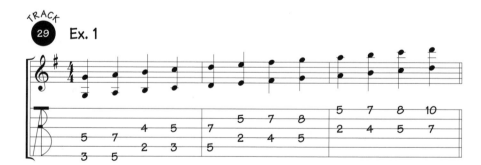

If you already know how to play two- or three-note bass runs between chords or you can keep a steady root-fifth fingerstyle thump going, you are familiar with some of the essential elements of bass playing, but once you get rid of the chords and melody and focus on the bottom groove, opportunities open up for more elaborate parts. Check out the familiar walking bass line (played in octaves) in Example 2. This might be a bit too complex to combine with standard chords, but when you play it separately it's a snap. Try playing just the low notes to get the feel of the part, then add the octave notes to fill out the sound. This is a pretty good workout for the fretting hand, so give your hand a rest by alternating between the low and high notes of each pair, as shown in Example 3.

Playing octaves like this works well with bass lines that dovetail neatly with the chord progression and don't compete with the melody. It's a particularly good approach when you are playing with several other guitars or with a keyboard instrument that is filling in the harmonic details. When you are the sole accompanist, though, you can get a little fancier. Let's look at a few parts that establish a contrasting groove or melody. Play the simple line in Example 4. The basic figure combines a little flurry of notes (similar to a bluegrass G run) followed by a quarter-note descending run. The part is defined by the chord changes, but it has a melodic motif of its own. In tandem with staccato rhythm guitar chops, this kind of line works particularly well with sustained vocals or legato guitar solos. You can hear similar riffs in such pop hits as the Temptations' "My Girl," the Beatles' "Day Tripper," and Spinal Tap's "Big Bottom."

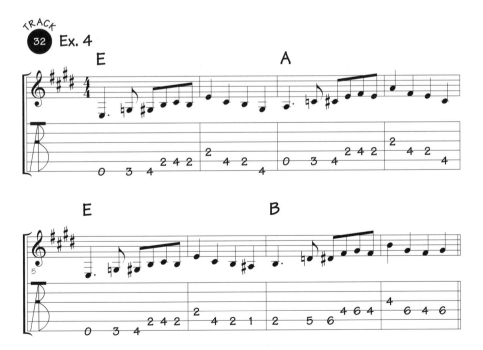

Now try the funky line on the lower staff of Example 5. The relatively busy bass riff is paired with a simple setting of a modal fiddle tune from West Virginia called "Sandy Boys." The interplay between the lead and the accompaniment is particularly fun in measures 4 and 6, where the ascending octave jumps in the bass contrast with the sustained A notes of the melody. This kind of backup line must be played in perfect rhythm to work well, and you'll need to convince the other rhythm players to play very sparsely so that your line will stand out. A simple offbeat chop or reggae skank will complement this line best.

To finish off, we'll play a loping, Latin-inspired bass line against a lively reel from the northern climes of Quebec: "Lévis Beaulieu." The Quebec fiddle style is incredibly bouncy and syncopated, and musicians frequently shift the accent of the phrases and alter the length of the notes to incorporate rests that vary the rhythm. The bass line I've added is syncopated in an entirely different way, and it is this juxtaposition of a lazy bass groove against the jaunty bounce of the fiddle tune that makes this so much fun to play. The accompaniment part, a repeating two-bar riff, is based on a Cuban son clave part and should be played with a relaxed feel. Notice that the third note in the pattern (the second A note in measure 1, for example) is tied across the bar line so that it rings into the second measure. Try damping the long notes very lightly with the palm of your picking hand, and then damp the quarter notes in the second measure a little more. In the B section (bars 10–18), the figure picks up a little steam and the part ends with a descending line (measures 16–18) that revisits the descending octave scale patterns we worked on earlier. Once you've got the pattern working like a well-oiled machine, try playing the first three notes in octaves.

You won't really need to get any more fancy than this to keep it fun and interesting. Finding the groove and drawing other players in is the essence of great bass playing, and the process of putting the right notes in exactly the right place is endlessly fascinating.

Lévis Beaulieu

Traditional, arranged by Paul Kotapish

Classic Pop Changes

Andrew DuBrock

I used to get grumpy when people would say that math and music go together. I'd argue that the interpretation and performance—the heart and soul—of music has nothing to do with math. I mean, if I showed up at the "Wild Thing" extendo-jam with my pocket protector and pencils, I'd be laughed out of the room!

But there are many aspects of music that do use numbers and simple mathematical relationships. If you've ever heard someone say "Just go to the IV chord," you were hearing a reference to the most basic use of math in music. Numbering chords is a good way to show their relationship to one another and to the underlying key of a song. In this lesson, we'll learn how to number the chords in a key and how to use that knowledge to play some classic chord progressions in a variety of different keys.

CHORD NUMBERS

There are seven notes in a major scale, and the chords that are built on top of them can be given numbers that correspond to the numbers of the steps of the scale. For example, the major scale in the key of C is illustrated below with each step numbered:

1	2	3	4	5	6	7	8
C	D	E	F	G	A	B	C

Notice that after the seventh step, you're back at C again—the pattern starts over as you go higher (or lower).

If you build triads (three-note chords) on top of these scale steps, you get a pattern of major, minor, and diminished chords that is the same in every key. Roman numerals are usually used to label chords, so the "one" chord is I, the "four" chord is IV, etc. Major chords are usually labeled with uppercase (IV) symbols and minor chords with lowercase (vi) ones, as indicated below:

1	2	3	4	5	6	7
Major	Minor	Minor	Major	Major	Minor	Diminished
I	ii	iii	IV	V	vi	vii°

Notice that the I, IV, and V chords are major and the ii, iii, and vi chords are minor. But what's that little circle after the vii° chord? That means it's a diminished chord, an odd beast that is used in classical music and some jazz but hasn't found its way into many pop songs. We won't worry about it in this lesson.

I, IV, AND V

The I, IV, and V chords are the meat and potatoes of chord progressions, and many songs never stray from these three chords. The progression in Example 1 strings these three chords together into the classic "La Bamba" progression.

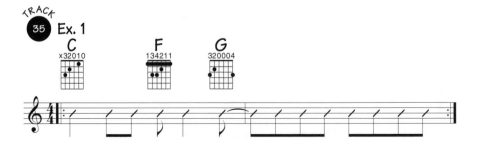

TRACK 35 Ex. 1

Another classic I–IV–V progression is the "Twist and Shout" progression in the key of A. The A-major scale is A, B, C♯, D, E, F♯, G♯, so the I–IV–V progression in A would be what? That's right: A, D, E (Example 2). Change the rhythm slightly and you end up with Buddy Holly's "Words of Love" progression in Example 3.

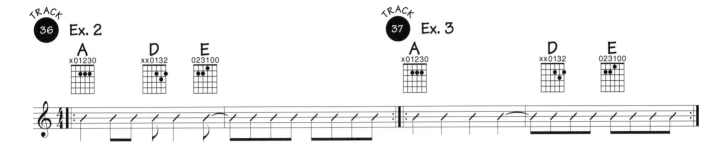

Another variation of this classic progression takes the I–IV–V and passes through the IV chord on the way back to I. The I–IV–V–IV progression in Example 4 is featured in such tunes as "Wild Thing." The classic "Good Lovin'" uses the same progression in D (Example 5).

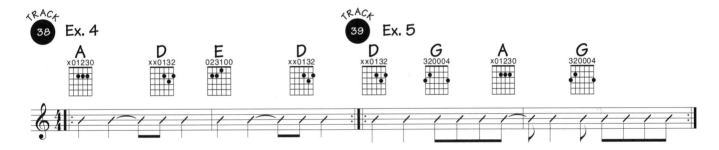

MINOR CHORDS

Now let's look at some classic progressions that use minor chords. The I–vi–IV–V progression can be found in numerous classic pop songs; in Example 6, we have it in the "Earth Angel" key of G. So what would the chords of a I–vi–IV–V progression be if we started on C? You can check to see whether you're right with Example 7's "Blue Moon" progression.

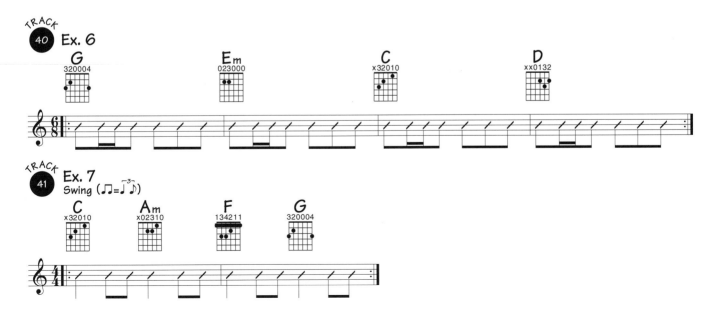

There are many variations on this popular progression. If you put the I chord between the IV and V, you get the vi–IV–I–V progression heard in songs like Sarah McLachlan's "Building a Mystery" (Example 8). Starting this one in a different place gives us U2's I–V–vi–IV "With or Without You" progression (Example 9).

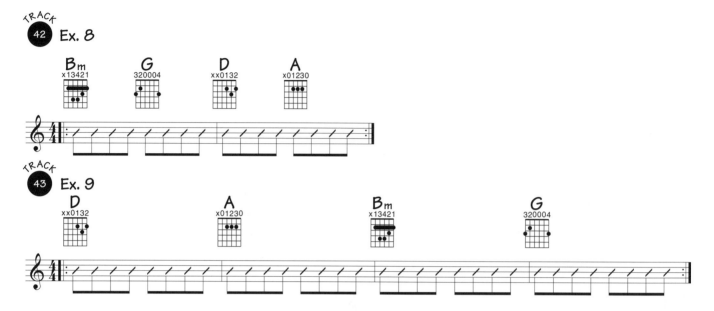

If you swap the IV in the I–vi–IV–V progression for a ii, you get another classic twist on the same progression: I–vi–ii–V. Example 10 shows this in the "You Send Me" key of G. Within this chord sequence is one of the most common short progressions: the ii–V–I progression that is found in all styles of music, especially jazz. Example 11 shows the opening progression of Sonny Rollins' "St. Thomas," which ends with ii–V–I (Dm–G–C).

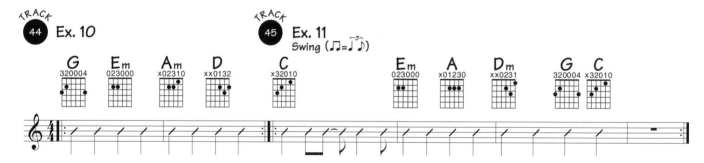

Now let's substitute the iii chord for the vi chord in the I–vi–ii–V progression. The Beatles used the I–iii–ii–V progression in Example 12 in the verses of "You're Going to Lose That Girl."

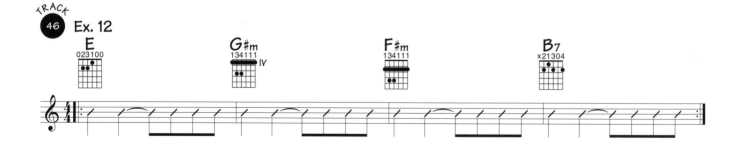

THE ♭VII CHORD

Instead of the vii° chord, many people use a ♭VII (flat seventh) chord, another major chord that is very common in classic rock as well as bluegrass tunes. In the key of D, for example, the seventh step of the D-major scale (D, E, F♯, G, A, B, C♯) is C♯. Lowering (or flatting) the C♯ gives us a C♮, illustrated in the I–♭VII–IV progression in Example 13, which is in the same key as "Sweet Home Alabama." The same progression is used in E in Van Morrison's "Gloria" (Example 14). Starting this progression on the ♭VII gives us the chorus to "With a Little Help from My Friends" (Example 15).

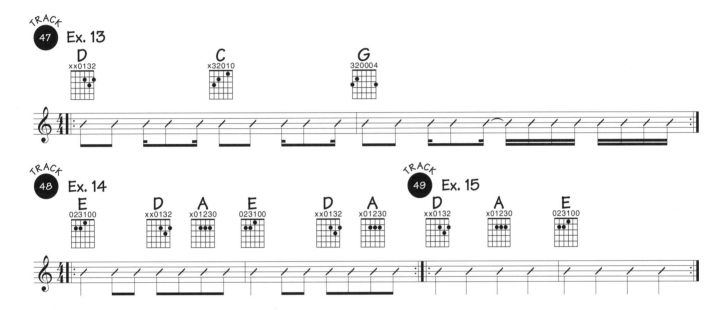

Swing Voice Leading

Tony Marcus

If you listen to the best practitioners of swing rhythm guitar, you'll notice (along with their propulsive 4/4 beat) that the chord progressions they use really hang together. Great rhythm players use voice leading to link each note in a chord with a corresponding note in the next chord. The result is a smooth flow that carries the tune along.

If you're used to playing barre chords, you may notice that in going from a barred G-major chord to a D7/A, (as in Example 1, below), you are going from six notes in the first chord to four notes in the second. You'll create a more cohesive sound if you substitute a four-note G6 chord for that barre chord (Example 2). Not only do you now have one four-note chord moving to another one, but that G6–D7/A change is an example of good voice leading. Notice how every note in the G6 chord in Example 2 moves a minimal distance to get to the note in the D7/A chord: the G in the bass goes up two frets to A, the fourth-string E also moves up two frets to become F#, the third-string B goes up just one fret to C, and the second-string D doesn't move at all.

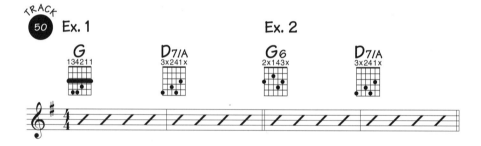

It might help if you think of your guitar as a collection of different instruments rather than one chord machine. If you listen to the horn section in a swing big-band recording, you'll notice that the arranger uses this same concept. In a harmonized section, each horn tends to move the least possible distance to the next note. It makes the music far more cohesive and pleasing to the ear.

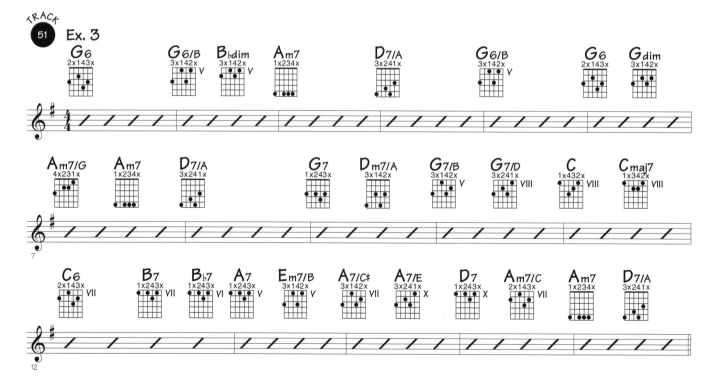

Let's put this idea to use. Example 3 shows the first 16 measures of a common chord progression you'd find in tunes like "Pennies from Heaven" and "I Can't Give You Anything but Love." Notice the voice leading in the second measure where the G6/B segues neatly into the B♭dim chord: two notes stay the same and the other two move down one fret. The same sort of movement gets you from the B♭dim to the Am7: the sixth and third strings go down one fret, while the second and fourth strings remain at the same pitch. Once you are able to play all the chord voicings in Example 3, listen to how the close resolutions lend a sound of continuity to the progression.

Notice that the Dm7/A chord in measure 9 is exactly the same shape as the G6/B in measure 2; it's just two frets lower on the neck. Many chords change name depending on how they're used. Let's look at the form in question. It can be viewed (from the bass note up) as the third, root, fifth, and sixth of a major chord or as the fifth, third, seventh, and root of a minor-seventh chord. When you get to more extended chord forms, it's not uncommon for one shape to be correctly labeled three or four different ways. For instance, a dominant-ninth chord (without root), a minor-sixth chord, and a minor-seventh flat five (half-diminished) chord all have the same notes.

Example 4 is a D-minor vamp you might play at the beginning of a song. It contains close-voiced, three-note chords rather than the more open four-note chords in the other examples. Played at a medium tempo, this sort of progression perfectly sets the mood for all sorts of minor-key tunes, including "I've Found a New Baby" and "It Don't Mean a Thing if It Ain't Got That Swing."

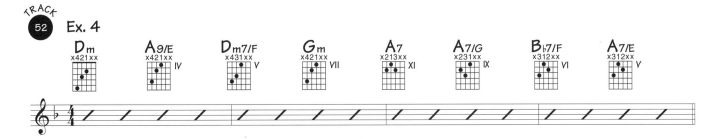

Example 5 explores the concept of connecting chords. Connecting chords are chords that might not have anything to do with the harmonic content of the song you're playing. Their sole purpose is to link together chords that do relate to the song's harmonic content. If you start and finish with the appropriate chord, the ear allows all sorts of liberties to be taken in between. In this case, I've used diminished chords, which don't imply any particular tonality. The basic progression here is G–G7–C–C9, and the diminished chords lead you nicely from one inversion to the next.

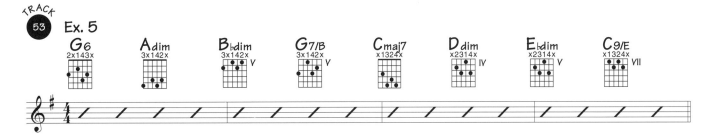

Once you've experimented with these progressions, you can seek out a more complete compendium of swing chords and experiment with linking various sorts of chord forms together with minimal movement. If this seems daunting, remember that these are all closed chords that can be moved anywhere on the fretboard. So a single shape can be used for many different chords depending on where you play it. An F7 on the first fret is a G7 on the third fret, an A7 on the fifth fret, and so on. Have fun!

Celtic Jigs
David Surette

Among the various types of tunes common in Celtic music, the jig seems to give guitarists (especially those not weaned on Irish or Scottish music) more difficulty than others. The steady diet of tunes and songs in 4/4 and 3/4 that you find in bluegrass and American folk sessions makes the 6/8 time of the jig seem baffling. But once you become accustomed to them, jigs are a welcome change from the endless stream of blazing reels that comprise many sessions these days.

While Ireland has quite possibly the largest, most varied, and most beautiful jig repertoire, some say that the jig rhythm was exported centuries ago to Ireland from Italy, where 6/8 rhythms such as saltarellos, tarantellas, and monferrines date back to medieval times. Of course, jigs are played today in many traditions, including those of Scotland, Brittany (France), Cape Breton and other parts of Canada, and New England. In this lesson, we'll examine one Irish jig that has become a standard in the New England contra dance scene, "Coleraine," and another from Italy, "Monferrine."

RIGHT-HAND TECHNIQUE

Although written in 6/8 time, the rhythmic emphasis of a jig falls on the first and fourth beats. It's possible to count them effectively as 1 2 3, 2 2 3, with a slight secondary emphasis on the third and sixth beats. To underline this central pulse, I suggest using a basic pick direction of down-up-down, down-up-down. Although there's some debate among jig players about the best picking pattern, the down-up-down pattern will imbue your playing with a stronger and more rhythmic feel. It may seem awkward at first, but after a while it will become natural.

Example 1 uses an open-position G-major scale in 6/8 time, with the down-up-down pattern indicated. Example 2 is another exercise, or melodic pattern, using the G scale. Both of these examples let you get used to the down-up-down picking pattern. You can play similar exercises in other keys as well. The most important keys for Celtic music are G, D, C, and A.

TRACK
54   Ex. 1
     G-major scale

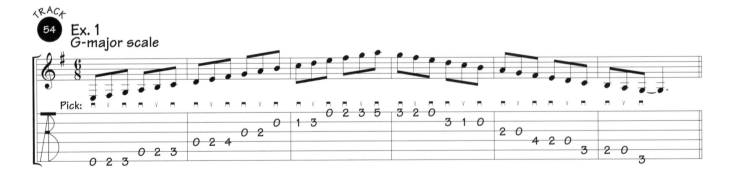

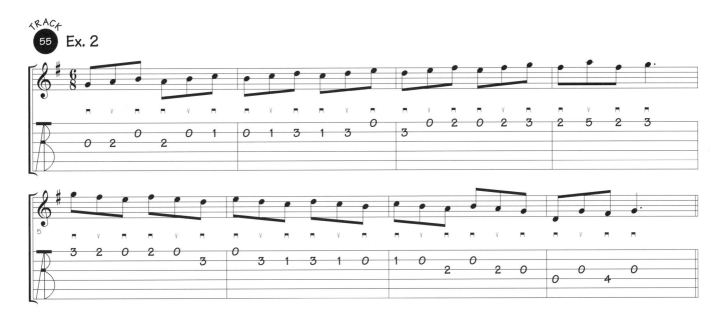

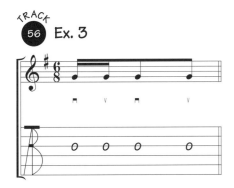

Along with the down-up-down pattern, the right-hand triplet is the other major technical element you'll need for playing Celtic jigs. Unless a hammer-on or pull-off is indicated in the notation, all three notes of a triplet should be picked with a down-up-down pick direction, as shown in Example 3. Even though they are called triplets, they actually sound (and are notated) as two 16th notes and an eighth note. The triplets take the place of the first two eighth notes of the first half measure, allowing you to then use an upstroke for the third eighth note. This may seem like a lot of thinking about pick direction, but once you internalize these moves, they'll become second nature. It is much easier to have a consistent way of picking than to try to reinvent the wheel every 16 bars.

PLAYING THE MELODIES

With these basic elements in mind, look at the final page of this lesson and try playing through "Coleraine" and "Monferrine." The Am-to-C movement in "Coleraine" is reminiscent of an Italian tarantella, making it a good partner with "Monferrine," which is the name of a kind of jig found in the Piedmont region of northern Italy. This one works quite well in New England contra dances. I recorded a mandolin version of this tune with fiddler Rodney Miller on our *New Leaf* CD.

For those new to jigs, I recommend working on the basic pick direction first. When you're comfortable with that, try adding in a few triplets here and there (in addition to those notated with 16th notes). You can execute a triplet by playing anywhere from one to three different pitches. Example 4 illustrates single-note, double-note, and triple-note triplets. Good taste, restraint, and listening to the way other traditional instruments ornament these tunes will help you develop your own style and approach.

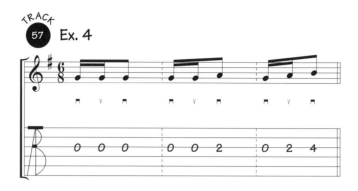

JIG BACKUP

Examples 5–7 show three different strum patterns you can use to play backup to these tunes. Each provides a different feel. Example 5 is the jig equivalent of a boom-chick pattern and one of the basic sounds of many New England contra dance pianists. It's very important that the bass note is played on beat 1 and the chord on beat 3; otherwise it starts to drift into 4/4 territory. For that unhip old-time sound, play both the boom and the chick with downstrokes.

Example 6 is the down-up-down picking pattern in strum form. If played lightly with a combination of notes and strums, it can be delicate and lovely. You can also use it as a powerful bash 'n' thrash style.

Example 7 is a syncopated groove that works as a counter-rhythm to the standard rhythm, and it has a more contemporary feel to it as well. It's important to note that the pick direction for this rhythm is different: it's now a down-up pattern, and the emphasis is on the first and third notes of the 6/8 measure. You can get a nice percussive effect by damping the strings slightly on these beats.

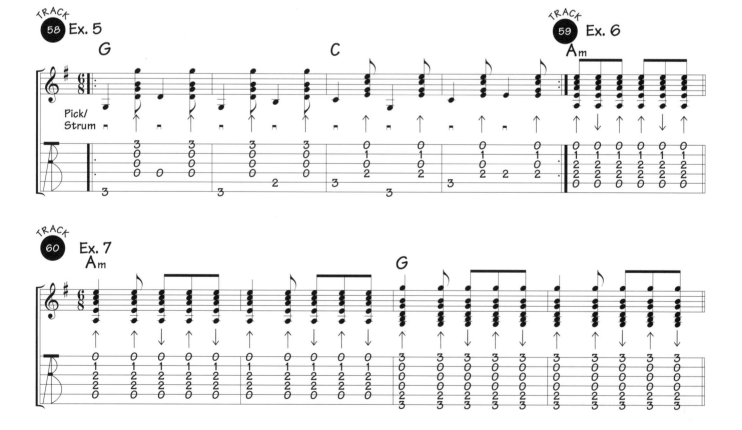

The somewhat more relaxed speed of jigs (six notes in the space of eight) makes them a good choice for guitarists working to keep pace with fiddlers. With a little practice, you'll soon be jamming along with the best of them.

Coleraine/Monferrine

Traditional, arranged by David Surette

Melodic Improvisation
Chris Grampp

To the uninitiated guitarist, improvisation appears to be a daunting task of creating musical ideas on the spot, often at high speed and over songs that the player may hardly know. For the great majority of musicians, however, nothing could be further from the truth. Improvising requires a thorough familiarity with the song; a reliance on scales, licks, and arpeggios; and loads of preparation and practice. There are very few people who can truly create original lines at a moment's notice. Most of us play variations of previously conceived ideas and are grateful when we occasionally create something truly original on the spot.

Like all types of music, improvised solos contain three ingredients: melody, harmony, and rhythm. Many jazz artists like to "run the changes," where the soloist plays arpeggios and scales common to the chord changes and key centers. This type of harmonic improvising can be intellectually challenging, but if carried too far, it may result in a solo that bears little resemblance to the original song. Some soloists play rhythmically, emphasizing syncopation and repeated figures separated by a regular sequence of rests. Beginners often find this to be the easiest type of improvising to learn, since rhythmic motifs can be created with very few notes. Perhaps the most pure type of improvisation occurs when the soloist uses the melody of the song as the basis for creating new ideas. Louis Armstrong was a genius at this approach; he was able to spin out endlessly fresh reinterpretations of any song while never losing sight of the melody.

In this lesson we'll explore the melodic basis of improvisation, using the traditional song "Red River Valley," which is mostly played as a folk song but is adaptable to many styles of music. I've played it as a folk song, a blues, a waltz, a bossa, and a jazz standard. Improvisation is not exclusive to jazz, blues, and rock 'n' roll, by the way; it is common in many styles of music.

SONG STRUCTURE

Many popular and traditional songs share similar chords, and without a theme to provide structure and identity, solos on these songs would begin to sound the same. It's important to identify the melodic structure and characteristics of a song in order to make your solo relate to it specifically. Play through the melody of "Red River Valley" in Example 1 below. Thoroughly knowing a song is the first requirement for being able to effectively solo on it, so if you're not already familiar with this tune, play "Red River Valley" until it becomes second nature.

TRACK 62 Ex. 1

Notice that the melody has a repeating theme. The first eight bars include a simple call-and-response pattern in which a phrase is stated and then answered with a slightly different phrase. Example 2 shows the theme in measures 1–8 expressed rhythmically. This rhythmic motif is repeated in the second half of the song (measures 9–16).

Ex. 2

EMBELLISHING THE MELODY

The first soloing technique we'll look at, which you may already be doing without knowing it, is one of the most common: embellishing the melody with grace notes, fills, passing tones, and rhythmic variations. Sticking close to the melody is the best preparation for eventually departing from it. There are countless ways to embellish the melody of "Red River Valley." Example 3 shows one.

TRACK 63 Ex. 3

Three basic things are going on in Example 3. First, I changed many of the half notes to a dotted quarter followed by an eighth note. The dotted quarter/eighth note combination still adds up to a half note, but it creates a syncopated or swing feel in which the dotted quarter note is drawn out until it nearly topples over onto the eighth note. This syncopation breaks up the regular feel of the melody and makes it groove. Example 4 illustrates this with an excerpt from measures 9–10.

TRACK 64 Ex. 4

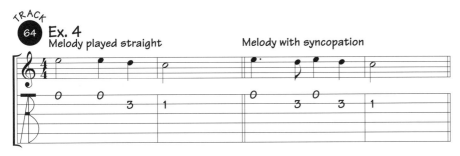

I also added eighth notes to Example 3 in some measures where a quarter or half note might otherwise be found. Example 5 illustrates how these additions vary the regular pattern of the melody in bars 6–7. As another form of embellishment, I added passing tones between the melody notes in many measures. Example 6 shows how I did this in measures 10–12.

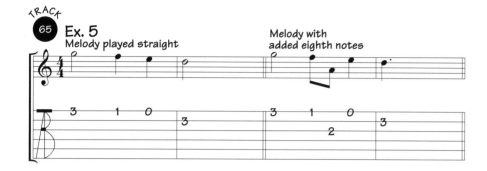

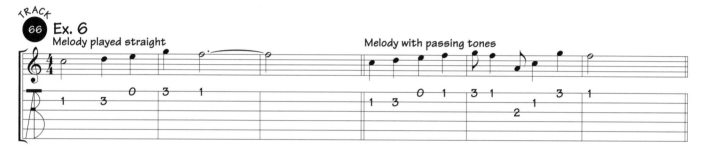

Finally, to complement the melody, I have added fills to portions of the melody where half or whole notes are found. Whole notes, half notes, and rests are excellent places to add embellishments, as they provide space for a counterpoint to the original tune. See measures 3–4 and 7–8 for examples.

Your next step is to play around with the melody of "Red River Valley" yourself for awhile. You may find, as I did, that the simple theme of the song is actually quite hard to alter. After you have worked at it for a bit, embellishments will start coming to you. Write them down or record them, and try to figure out why certain things work and others do not.

VARYING THE MELODY

Next, let's create some melodic variations to "Red River Valley." We'll begin by breaking the song down into four-bar sections and listening carefully to the melody and rhythm of each section. Go back and study Example 2, because the rhythmic structure shown there will be the basis for our variations.

Examples 7–10 show the four-bar alterations of the melody I came up with. I started by singing the melody to myself and then singing variation after variation until I came up with melodies I liked. Then I refined them by playing them on the guitar. The variations are without embellishment and sound a bit wooden. They are only the raw material that we will use to build musical phrases.

EMBELLISHING THE MELODIC VARIATIONS

Now comes the fun part! We are going to embellish the variations with passing tones and syncopations just as we did in Examples 4–6. This will make the new lines sound less wooden and technical (and more fun to play). Go ahead and apply the techniques we previously used to each of your favorite phrases from Examples 7–10. You should now have four embellished four-bar phrases that you can string together into one single, uninterrupted solo. The solo I came up with is shown in Example 11. Compare this with your own solo to see alternate ways of embellishing the lines. These aren't improvised solos in the literal sense, since they were not created by ear on the spot. But they represent the sort of preparation needed to create melodically based ideas as you play.

This approach to soloing can be applied to almost any song. In the beginning, it is important to note your musical ideas on paper or tape. Notation not only preserves your ideas for future use; it gives you the chance to mold them into their best incarnation. Eventually you will find these ideas creeping into your playing spontaneously. This is where you start reaping the rewards of all your preparation, and soloing gets to be really fun.

Soloing with Arpeggios

By Jamie Findlay

When a musician improvises, he or she is spontaneously creating a melody in much the same way that a composer creates a melody. The composer and improviser use the same tools—scales, arpeggios, and modes—to craft their music; the difference is that the composer has all the time in the world to create a melody, and the improviser has to do it now! So the improviser needs to have the basic tools in his or her hands to successfully address the harmonic situations that occur in different musical settings. One of the most difficult and rewarding challenges in jazz is learning how to solo in a way that follows the chord changes. In this lesson, we'll focus on using arpeggios as a soloing tool, using a couple of jazz/blues progressions.

Example 1 is a basic blues progression in B♭—a common key for jazz instruments like the trumpet and tenor saxophone—but you can also try playing all the ideas in this lesson in other keys. Play the chords with an even four strokes to the bar—Freddie Green style—to get the sound of the changes in your head.

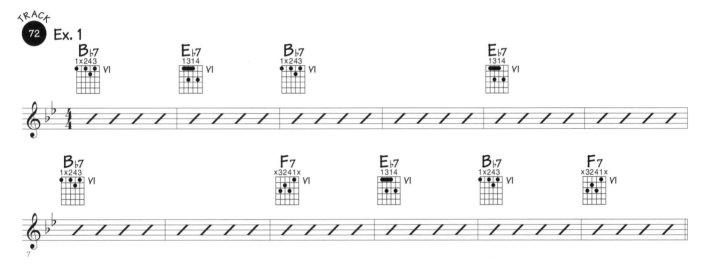

Next move on to Example 2, which is an example of eighth-note arpeggio patterns that match the changes. The first measure is a B♭7 arpeggio, derived from the B♭7 chord shape in Example 1, which follows the notes of the chord (root, third, fifth, seventh) from bottom to top and across the fretboard from the sixth string to the second string. The second measure is the same dominant-seventh pattern but this time over the E♭7 chord, starting with the root on the fifth string. In measures 3–4 and 5–6 the chord lasts for two bars so the ascending arpeggio pattern is followed by a descending pattern using the same notes. Notice that the F7 arpeggio in measures 9 and 12 is the same as the E♭7 but moved up two frets. Play through the whole example slowly at first and then build it to a moderate tempo.

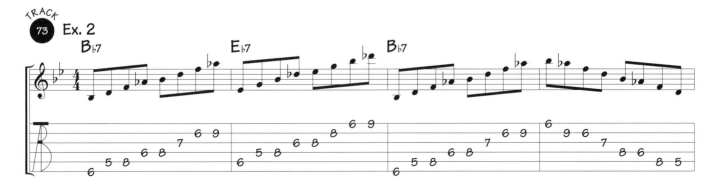

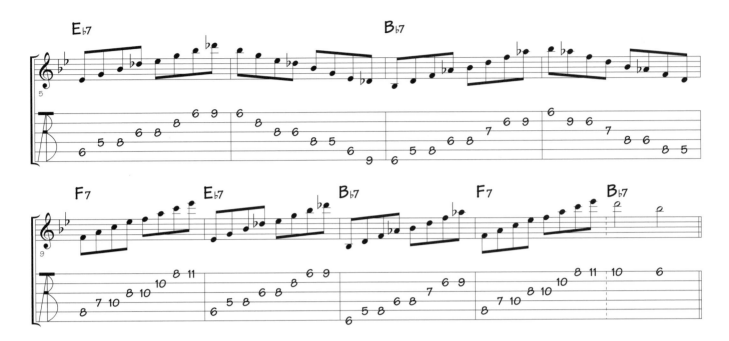

Example 3 is similar to Example 2, but it starts with descending arpeggios instead of ascending. Notice that in bars 7 and 8, the B♭7 arpeggio starts on the third of the chord. The third is probably the most important note in the chord because it identifies the chord as being either major or minor. It is also a strong melodic tone because it doesn't exist in the preceding chord in this progression. I also used a different F7 arpeggio, beginning on the low A note (the third of F7), in measure 12 on the turnaround. I like the way it sounds, although it's a little more challenging. Notice how the B♭ note at the end of measure 11 moves smoothly into the A note that begins measure 12.

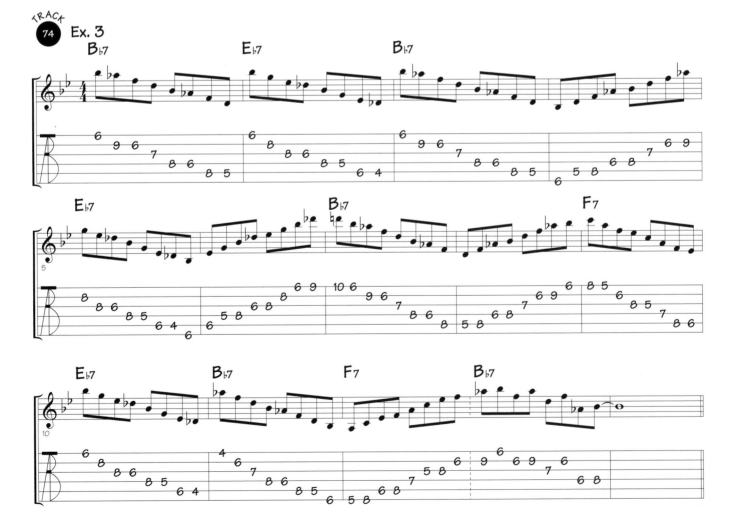

Understanding the way a chord progression moves and the way notes from one chord resolve into the next is very helpful when improvising. Look at the B♭7 and E♭7 chords below:

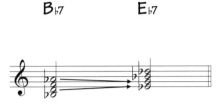

The B♭7 chord is spelled B♭, D, F, A♭, and the E♭7 is spelled E♭, G, B♭, D♭. There are some notes in the B♭7 that can move chromatically to the notes in E♭7: the A♭ note in B♭7 can move to the G note in E♭7, and the D note in B♭7 can move to the D♭ note in E♭7. This is called chromatic movement, and it creates a sense of forward momentum. Example 4 illustrates this concept quite dramatically. The A♭ of B♭7 at the end of measure 1 goes smoothly into the G of E♭7 at the beginning of measure 2. The same goes for the A to B♭ in bars 2–3 and the D♭ to D♮ in bars 6–7.

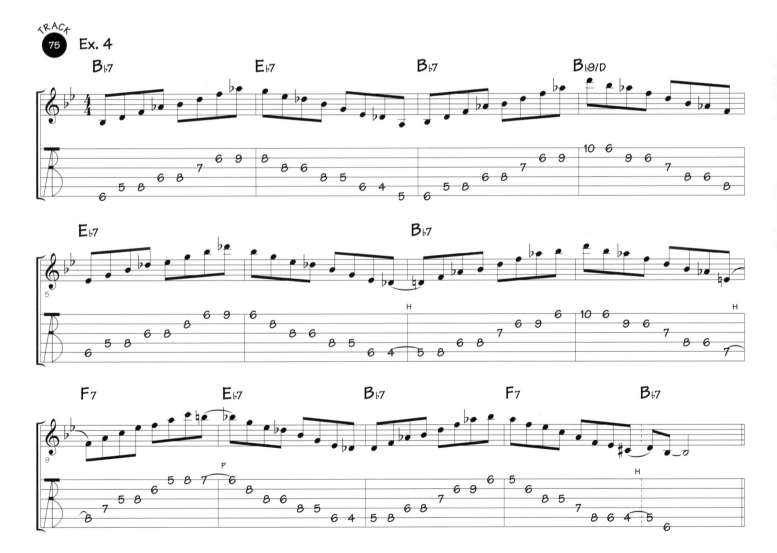

The chord progression in Example 5 is more of a jazz/blues progression, one that you might find in a fake book or hear on a mainstream jazz recording. You'll notice that there's more movement in the chords. This is what jazz harmony is all about—chord substitution and good voice leading. The second measure includes an Edim7 chord that leads nicely back to the B♭9 (notice how the E note resolves to the fifth of the B♭7, F). In the fourth measure, a ii7–V7 (Fm7–B♭7) progression sets up the E♭9 chord in the fifth measure. And in bar 6, a whole measure of Edim7 gets you back to B♭7. Instead of using IV–V–I at the end of the progression, most jazz composers use ii–V–I, and I'll set that up by using a iii–VI (Dm7♭5–G7♭9) into the ii–V (Cm11–F7). You'll notice, however, that I've substituted an Adim7 chord for the F7, which takes us back to the I, B♭7. The progression ends with a turnaround (B♭7–Bdim7–Cm7–F7♭9) that sets up the beginning again.

Play through the progression a few times. It'll get you used to the sound of the chords and will get you ready to hear the arpeggios in the final example.

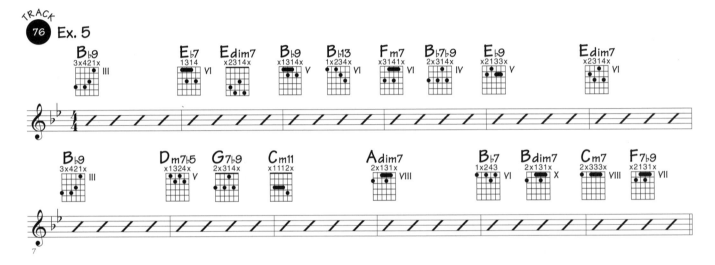

Example 6 begins with a four-note B♭7 arpeggio, followed by a four-note Dm7♭5 arpeggio, which creates a B♭9 sound. Notice how similar the Dm7♭5 arpeggio is to the B♭7. In measure 2, the four-note E♭7 arpeggio is followed by a four-note Edim7 arpeggio. The diminished-seventh chord/arpeggio is often used by improvisers and composers because it gives you another note that can resolve smoothly into the next chord. In this case the seventh of the Edim7 chord (C♯) resolves up a half step into the D in the B♭7 chord.

Measure 4 uses arpeggios that follow the Fm7–B♭7♭9 progression to resolve to the E♭9 in bar 5. The B♭7♭9 arpeggio does not contain a root. It starts on the third of the chord and is in fact the same as a Ddim7 arpeggio (D, F, A♭, C♭). Notice how the last note in the Fm7 arpeggio (E♭) moves smoothly down a half step into the D note in the B♭7♭9 arpeggio.

The next three measures use descending and ascending arpeggios to outline the basic chords (E♭7, Edim7, B♭7). Notice how the notes at the end of the measures resolve into the next arpeggio. Half-step resolutions always sound smooth and work really well.

Measure 8 is a ii7–V7 progression (Dm7♭5–G7♭9) that resolves to Cm11. One of my favorite colors for a minor chord is the minor 11th. Measure 9 starts with a descending Cm7 arpeggio and adds the 11th (F note) in the second half of the measure.

In measure 10, the Adim7 (A, C, E♭, G♭) is a substitution for the F7 chord (an A♭dim7 arpeggio is almost identical to an F7♭9 arpeggio—F, A, C, E♭, G♭). The line starts on the flatted ninth of the F7 chord and descends. The last note—the flatted seventh (E♭) of the F7 chord—resolves into the third (D) of the B♭7 chord in the next measure.

The next two-bar collection of four-note arpeggios (measures 11–12) is the final turnaround. Turnarounds are often found at the end of a chorus of music, or the end of the form of a song, and are designed to set up the next section. This turnaround, often referred to as a I–vi–ii–V progression, is quite common, although in this instance the vi chord (G minor) is replaced with a Bdim7 chord. This can be played in pretty much the same position on the neck; you'll just need to shift down to get the A♭ in the first measure. All the rest of it fits in the fifth position. Turnarounds are very common in jazz and having a good vocabulary of them is a must for any improviser. Measure 13 finishes off the solo with a bluesy B♭7 arpeggio riff that outlines some of the extensions of the dominant chord.

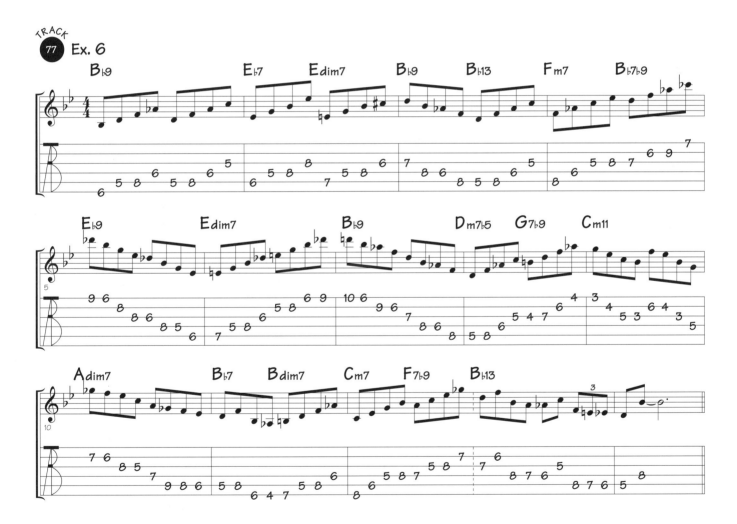

We've come pretty far pretty fast in this lesson. Take the time to ingest this information slowly and in small chunks, and it should open up a whole new way of playing for you.

Getting Low Lows with a Partial Capo

Peter Mulvey

TRACK
78 Tune-up: B A D G B E
Partial Capo IV, Strings 1–5

Partial capo techniques can broaden the already broad range of the guitar. I first encountered the technique years ago when my friend Joe used its most common form: capoing strings 1–5 at the second fret and playing D chord shapes above it. This let him play in E with a dropped-D effect without altering the tuning. There are many such possibilities: for example, capo strings 1–5 at the seventh fret and play an Am chord shape. You get a big, fat Em chord.

My own take on this technique involves altering the tuning of the bass string to exaggerate the effect, and it blossomed during a gig at the Wintertide Coffeehouse on Martha's Vineyard. There were two other guitar players performing "Time of the Season" by the Zombies in the key of F♯m, and they asked me to join them. In order to avoid being redundant by playing in their range, I capoed the top five strings of my guitar at the fourth fret and tuned down a whole step from standard, and then I lowered my uncapoed sixth string all the way down to F♯. This gave me "open" strings F♯ B E A C♯ F♯, low to high. It allowed me to play a cool bass line in their key and still stay out of their way. I was so delighted by this tuning that I used it in a song, "If Love Is Not Enough," which would go on to gain me some notice.

I've gone on to use the technique in several other songs as well. Dropping the uncapoed sixth string way down gives me a bass note that will come in handy with whatever I'm doing on the capoed strings. This technique extends what the guitar is already good at. A guitar has a very broad range of notes that are easy to play together. For example, in standard tuning, the lowest G (third fret, sixth string) and a G two octaves up (third fret, first string) are separated by only one and a half inches of fingerboard. This is exciting stuff! Alternate tunings, which usually involve lowering the bass strings, accentuate this strength. This kind of partial capoing just goes a step further down that path. Here's an example to get you going.

Put your guitar in standard tuning at standard pitch. Capo strings 1 through 5 at the fourth fret, and drop the sixth string down to B, five half steps from its original E pitch. Notice that when you leave the sixth string open and form the upper part of a G-chord shape on the capoed strings you get a big major chord with a low, growly bass root.

B
010034 Capo IV

Although it looks like a G, it sounds as a B-major chord, just as it would if you capoed all six strings at the fourth fret and played a G-chord shape. But this time, the bass note is an octave lower.

Strum or fingerpick this chord using any pattern you like, and then try adding the dominant seventh (A) by fretting the fourth string three frets above the capo.

B7
012034 Capo IV

This chord sounds great with Example 1, a fingerpicking pattern ripped off from Leo Kottke.

Ex. 1

Tuning: B A D G B E, Partial Capo IV, Strings 1–5

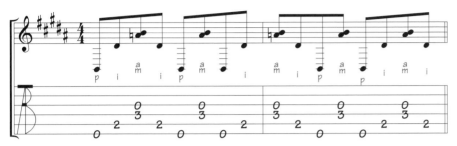

After four measures, go to the IV chord, E major, using a C shape on the capoed strings.

E

T3201x *Capo IV*

The root of this chord is now right under your thumb, at the first fret above the capo. You can also form an E7 chord by fretting the third string three frets above the capo.

E7

T324xx *Capo IV*

Play two measures of this chord, return to the I chord for a couple of measures, and then look for the V chord. (By now you've probably noticed that we're building a 12-bar blues structure. It's not a searingly original thing, but this is a unique window into it.) The V chord is a D7 shape, but the bass note is three frets above the capo at the seventh fret, and the chord really sounds as an F♯7.

F♯7

30021x *Capo IV*

Play a measure of this, a measure of the IV chord, a measure of the I, then the V chord for the turnaround, and you've got the basic blues form loved and abused by so many (see Example 2 on next page).

This technique does have some restrictions, and one of them becomes evident when you try to play the II chord, C♯ (an A shape). Try it. You're in trouble, right? The bass note you want is down below the capo, at the second fret. You can get to it, but then you have no way to form the chord on top of it; it's four frets above with a capo stuck in between! The only available bass note is the open capoed fifth string, which takes you out of the low bass range. In other words, this technique makes some things possible and others impossible (or at least awkward), thus nudging your creative process in a given direction.

Another good thing about this tuning is that it creates separate entities out of the bass and treble and teaches you to address them that way in normal tunings, which is often enlightening. And finally, the lower the bass string gets, the more low end comes through the speakers and straight to the bones of your audience.

TRACK 80 Ex. 2

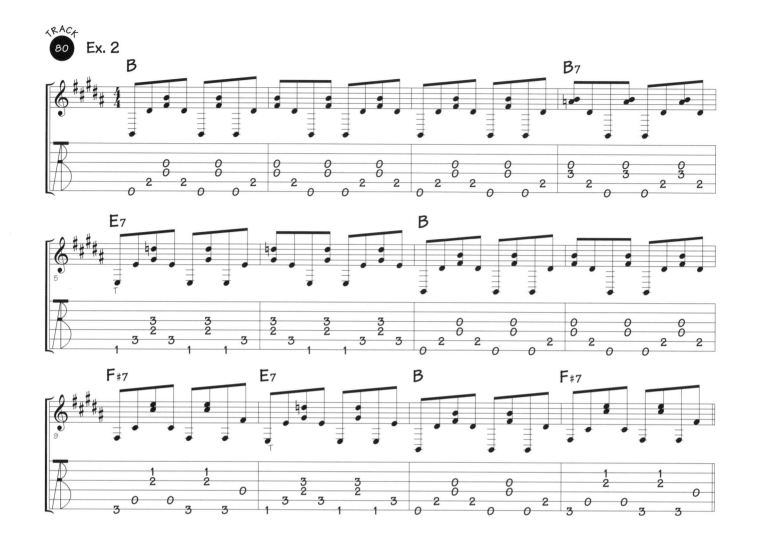

Hawaiian Slack Key
Keola Beamer

Most of us out here in the Hawaiian Islands are familiar with the way of slack. For 2,000 years our ancestors have looked out over the vastness of the Pacific Ocean. There are nights under these stars when the sequined movement of that ocean sings to us. Revealed in that beautiful whispering is a simple truth: life is short. So we slack down our lives, have a little fun, and play from the heart. We also slack down the strings of our guitars to match the tone of our lifestyles, and that's why our unique guitar style is called slack key.

Hawaiians like myself refer to the sound *of ki ho'alu* (slack key) as *nahenahe*, a soft, satisfying sound that wafts in the air like the fragrance of an awapuhi lei. To us, *nahenahe* is both a sound and a state of being. To discover the sound, you may have to break a few established rules and rethink the nature of the instrument while at the same time respecting its traditions.

There are roughly 40 tunings that we play in, and the way of slack matches the tuning to the source material. Since each tuning has its own unique coloration, timbre, and technical challenges, we are gifted with a world of choices. Every time we slack to a new tuning, we deconstruct the familiar and we are children again. We make mistakes, but we laugh a lot and are not too hard on ourselves. In the way of slack, there is nothing more useless than unyielding self-criticism—except of course the standard E A D G B E guitar tuner! You'll need a chromatic tuner (or better yet, your own ears) to get out there in the deep water.

Generally our tunings are divided into two main categories: male and female. Major tunings are ("see my fine war club") male; major-seventh and more esoteric, mysterious tunings are ("smile demurely, place flower in hair, run and hide in the bushes") female. The *wahine*, or female, tunings can get pretty fascinating. Let's take a look at a couple of pieces that use *wahine* tunings.

"A Grandmother's Wish" is a piece based on a lick that was taught to me by Auntie Alice Namakelua, who learned it from her brother, one of the first *paniolos* (cowboys) of old Hawaii. In this tuning, the top four strings are slackened a whole step, but the fifth and sixth strings are raised. Surprise! Not all strings are loosened. Auntie Alice taught me this one with the understanding that I would pass it on when it became my time to teach.

 TRACK 81 **Tune-up: B♭ Wahine, F B♭ C F A D**
^ ^ ∨ ∨ ∨ ∨

The form of the piece may differ a bit from other material you may be used to. The first part of the tune has five bars instead of the standard four. This is the way that Auntie Alice taught it to me and the way I grew to like it. I think early Hawaiian players would simply play the way they felt, without worrying about counting bars. Another common practice in slack-key music is repeating the vamp and tonic resolution throughout the piece, as in bars 4–5 and bars 10–11. I suspect this comes from the art of hula, where the dancers require symmetry and balance and move from one side to the other.

Let the bass notes sustain throughout this piece, with the treble riding sweetly on top. In the first two measures, try to play the hammer-ons cleanly. The tendency is to rush them, so make sure to stay relaxed and play them in time. Connect the notes together in the scalar passage in measure 3, crescendo to the top of the phrase, and accent the last note. Then move smoothly to the sixth-string bass in the following measure. At the end of measure 5, follow the repeat back to the beginning of the piece and then continue to the end. (We don't say the word *end* in Hawaii, by the way; we say *pau*.)

In the second part of the piece, continue to play the notes in a smooth, connected fashion. Measure 8 begins with a high phrase, which is played with the index and ring fingers of your left hand. Give the high notes a little vibrato by moving this two-note chord shape from side to side. In the second part of measure 8, slide the same chord shape down two frets and use vibrato again. In measure 9, the hammer-ons sound nice if you keep your fingers down on the notes after they are executed. (Try playing it without holding them down to see how choppy and awful this sounds!)

A Grandmother's Wish

Music by Keola Beamer and Auntie Alice Namakelua

"Wa'apa" is in G-*wahine* tuning, which is sometimes called *double slack*. This is because we normally get there in two steps. First, go to taro-patch tuning (D G D G B D) and then tune the third string down one half step to F♯. The note to play "with aloha" at the start of the piece is a reminder to play from the heart. In measure 1, you can either play the D as a hammer-on from nowhere, fretting and playing the F♯ note afterward, or you can play both the D and F♯ notes as hammer-ons from nowhere. I prefer the second option, but it is entirely up to you. In measures 2 and 4 (and later), roll the ring, middle, and index finders of your right hand to get a smooth sound from the 16th notes. Measures 1 and 2 are a vamp that repeats several times during the song, so spend a few minutes trying to play them smoothly.

The melody starts in measure 5, with a half barre in the fifth position. Barre only the treble strings so you can play the open bass strings to accompany the high melody. Go ahead and barre on the first beat, then reach out for the melody notes from your half barre position. Try to play the bass without hesitation and you'll start to express yourself in the way of slack. That alternating bass is one of the characteristic sounds of *ki ho'alu*. Keeping that uninterrupted bass going beneath the melody is also one of the trickiest aspects of the style. The low C is sustained for all of measures 13 and 17. Let the eighth notes in the melody ring together. In measures 14 and 18, hammer onto the high G with your pinky and then pull off to the index-finger E on the second fret.

Wa'apa

Music by Keola Beamer

+ **Hammer-on from nowhere**

I hope you've enjoyed this exploration of slack-key guitar and gotten a taste of Hawaii's beautiful and different music. These tunings and techniques will add wonderful flavors to your repertoire.

Classical Etude Variations
Mark Small

Through the centuries, composers such as Fernando Sor, Dionysio Aguado, Ferdinando Carulli, Mauro Giuliani, Heitor Villa-Lobos, and Leo Brouwer penned hundreds of études (studies) to help classical guitarists develop their technique. Today, guitarists of all stripes—classical players as well as steel-string instrumentalists—use them to develop speed and dexterity in their left and right hands. But some études, however beautiful and valuable, are so difficult to understand musically that many players are not able to benefit from the technique lessons they teach. Savvy students can derive maximum benefit from a single, playable étude by altering it to serve their personal technical needs.

Let's explore the "Prelude" by Ferdinando Carulli. This piece works well as a right-hand exercise because each chord lasts for a full bar, enabling you to apply a range of techniques to the chord progression. As you work with this—or any other—étude, strive to memorize the chord progression so you can free yourself from the page and think more about your right hand.

Before adapting what Carulli wrote, play through the original piece and see what techniques it can help you to improve. It's a nice, block-chord workout for both the left and right hands. I have written a target tempo of 160 beats per minute even though Carulli's moderato marking would be slower than that—probably 120 beats per minute at the fastest. From a strictly musical perspective, this piece has many unexpected harmonic turns. There are momentary modulations to B minor (bar 16), G major (bars 22–29), G minor (bar 30), E♭ (bar 32), A minor (bar 38), D minor (bar 42), and C major

(bar 44) via a series of colorful diminished chords. Note that I filled in the chords in bars 9–17 and 24–29, which originally contained three-note chord voicings, so that the whole piece could be played with four-note chord voicings.

Prelude
Music by Ferdinando Carulli

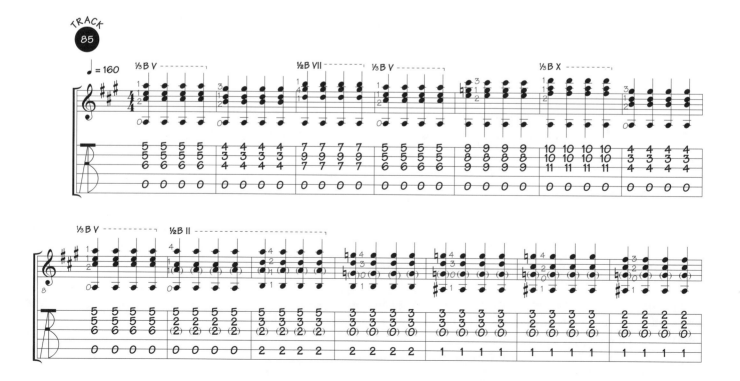

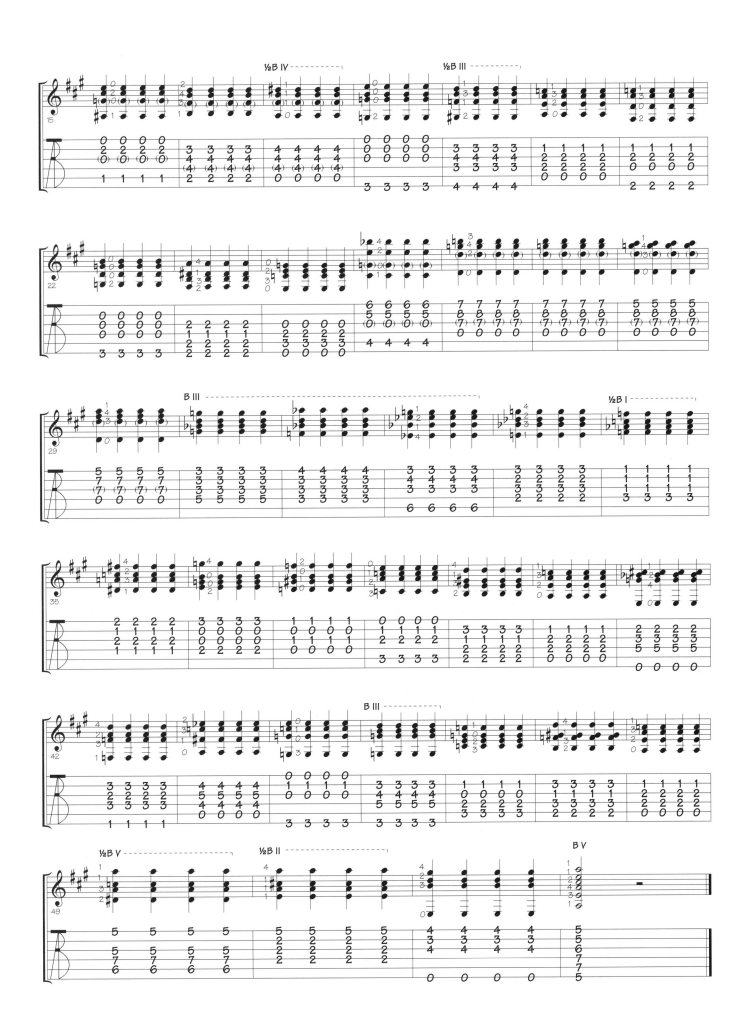

After playing the music as written, try exploring different combinations of right-hand fingerings to get a sense of how the individual voices move. Start by playing the bass line and then the two middle voices with *p*, *i*, and *m* (thumb, index, and middle fingers) as shown in Example 1.

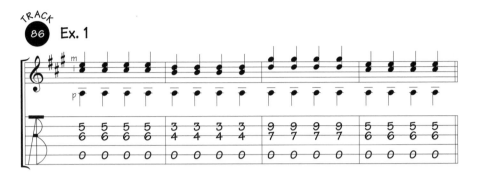

Then play through the piece again, ignoring the top note until you get to bars 9–17 and 25–29, where the original piece contained three-note voicings. Play those bars without the notes in parentheses and then drop from the top voice to the second voice when you reach bar 18. Do the same when you reach bar 30. You can also play only the bass line and top line as shown in Example 2.

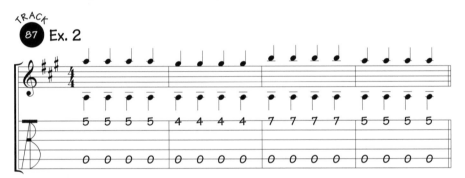

Next, let's change the right-hand pattern to a triplet arpeggio form (Example 3). Ironically, this is one of the most basic right-hand arpeggio patterns, yet it takes a lot of control to keep all of the notes even and unrushed.

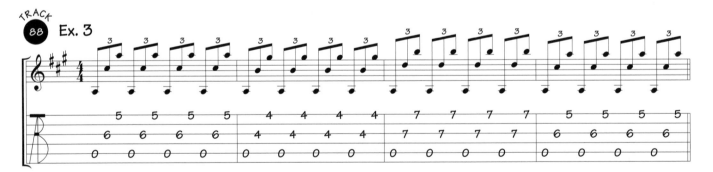

Now let's go back to the plucked chord approach and start changing things. Every voice of the chords should sound at the same volume. After playing it straight again, try rolling every chord as shown in Example 4. You might not perform a piece in this manner, but it's a great exercise for getting your rolled chords to sound even.

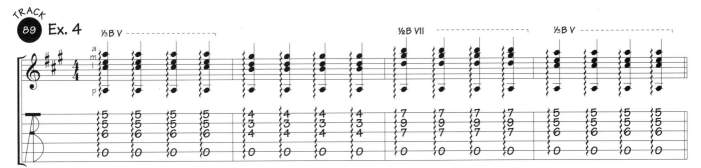

We'll use the four-note chords for the rest of this lesson to work various right-hand variations. Start by playing through the progression with 16th-note arpeggios (Example 5). This is another basic right-hand arpeggio pattern that is difficult to play in a controlled manner. Continue this pattern and play through the entire piece. The goal of this exercise is to keep every note rhythmically even and at a consistent volume. This variation quickly begins to feel like an endurance test!

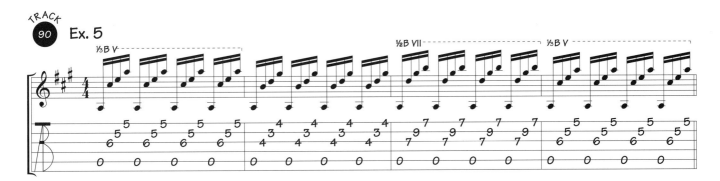

Let's continue with 16th notes but reverse the pattern as shown in Example 6. This is a bit more difficult to execute. Keep in mind that your primary goal is not speed, but clarity and an even rhythmic flow.

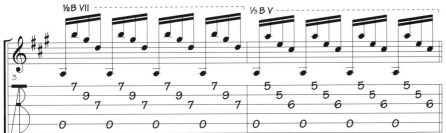

Example 7 employs sextuplets to create another common but challenging arpeggio form. Try playing these figures at slow, medium, and fast tempos to discover where your right hand feels most in control and where it seems to have the least control.

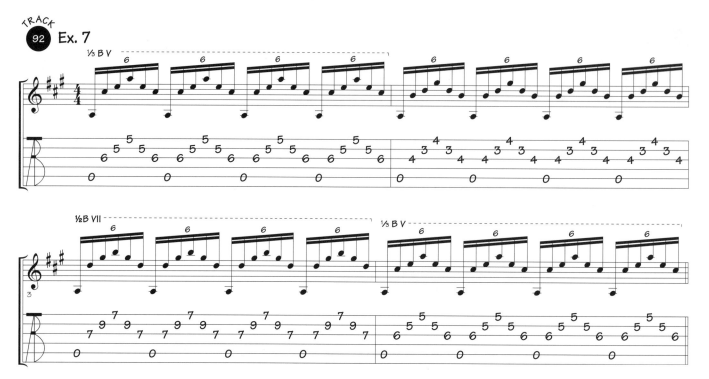

These ideas barely scratch the surface of what you can do with a single étude. Although developing your ability to read music is vitally important, this method will help you hone your right-hand technique using pieces you already know. Once you master an étude, try making up your own variations as we've done in this lesson. It can help you become more musically creative while providing a custom-made warm-up routine that targets the specific technical problems you want to overcome.

Modal Harmony

Scott Nygaard

In traditional Western triad-based harmony, chords are constructed by stacking thirds on top of each other: a minor third (a step and a half) stacked on top of a major third (two whole steps) gives you a major chord, and a major third atop a minor third is a minor chord. Even the "fancy" chords used in jazz and contemporary music, such as maj7, m11, 13, and even 7♭9, are constructed by stacking thirds on top of other thirds. Keep adding thirds on top of the 1, 3, and 5, and you get the 7, 9, 11, and 13. In the key of C, for example, you could add the B, D, F, and A notes to the 1, 3, and 5 of a C-major chord (C, E, and G). Notice that if you arrange all those notes (C, E, G, B, D, F, and A) in a slightly different order, you get a C-major scale: C, D, E, F, G, A, B.

In the music of many cultures around the world, the melody or rhythm is traditionally more important than the harmony. And in many instances, Western-influenced chord structures have been imposed upon what was originally scale- or mode-based music. Irish traditional music is a good example. This music originated with voice and bagpipes, and the addition of chordal instruments like piano and guitar is a relatively recent development. But the tunes didn't always take well to triad-based chord accompaniment, and this is one reason that Irish guitarists have often favored the droney sound of D A D G A D tuning, which allows them to accompany the tunes without using obvious triadic chord sounds. A similar thing happened in jazz in the '50s when Miles Davis and John Coltrane conceived of basing their solos and the backing harmonies of a tune on a scale, rather than on standard chords.

In this lesson, we'll explore the kinds of chords you can create by using the notes of the scale that corresponds to a given key. Forming chords by combining the notes of a scale in different ways is a great technique guitarists can use to find interesting new colors. Once you're freed from having to define a chord with specific notes—the root, the seventh, and the third—the options become endless.

To keep our fingers from getting tied in knots, we'll start by using an open string, D, as the root of the chord and play chords only on the three strings above it. Of course, to construct chords using a scale, you'll have to be familiar with the scale, not only across the fingerboard but up and down it as well. Example 1 shows triads in the key of D, with a D bass note, in which the voices in each chord move up the D scale step by step. For example, the notes on the third string move from A to B to C♯ to D to E to F♯ to G and back to A. The notes on the second string are clearly a D-major scale: D, E, F♯, G, A, B, C♯, D. If you're not seeing this as you play the chords, play single notes on each string one at a time, as in Example 2.

We'll start our exploration of modal chords by simply changing one note of the chord forms in Example 1. Let's try raising the F♯ in the first voicing to a G note. If we raise the highest note in all the voicings, we get Example 3. The notes on the second and third strings remain the same, but the notes on the first string are one scale step higher than in the voicings in Example 1. These particular voicings are often used in modal jazz and are sometimes called *fourth* chords, because they consist of fourths stacked on top of each other. Look at the first voicing: the interval from the A to the D is a fourth and the interval from the D to the G is also a fourth. The voicing on beat 4 of measure 1 sounds odd, doesn't it? As we do these exercises, we'll come upon chord voicings that may not seem to be very useful. But by going through every voicing of every configuration, we can learn what sounds good and what doesn't.

Next let's alter the first voicing by moving the middle voice, the D note, down a step, to the C♯. This chord sounds a little strange, but keep moving up the scale and see what nice chords we uncover with this configuration (Example 4).

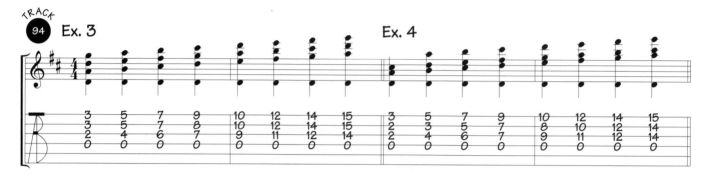

Example 5 moves the lower voice, the A note, up a step to a B. Now we're starting to get somewhere. Notice that each of the voicings contains a second interval—the B–C♯ in the first voicing, the C♯–D in the second, etc. Using seconds in chords is easy and common on the piano but rather difficult on the guitar. You'll most likely have to play the second and fifth voicings in Example 5 by stretching your index finger and pinky (or ring finger, if you've got big hands) three frets. And you'll have to make sure that the finger playing the note on the third string doesn't damp the note on the second string. These kinds of chords are very cool, and they would be much harder to pull off if you had to finger more than three notes.

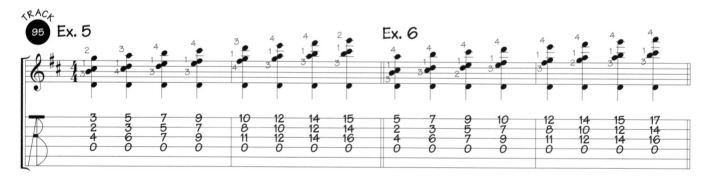

For some more piano like chords, let's raise the voicing on the first string by another step (Example 6). Ouch! These will take some work at first, and you'll need to make sure that your fretting-hand thumb is placed behind and in the middle of the neck. If you're used to wrapping your thumb around the neck, you'll have trouble playing these chords. But since you're only fretting three treble strings, you won't need as much strength in your whole hand. Before you feel like your tendons are going to burst, let's try another set of piano-ish chords that don't require quite so much stretching. Going back to our original voicing, let's raise the upper voice a step to a G and the middle voice a step to an E (Example 7).

I've been pretty systematic in my approach to finding these chords, but once you start to see where the notes of the scale are, you can create chords out of any of these notes, limited only by what sounds good to you and what your fingers can reach. Notice that I haven't given these chords a name. When forming chords modally, it's a little silly to worry about their names. For example, the first chord in Example 6 could be called a Dmaj13 or a Bm9/D or an Aadd9/D, none of which really tells you what notes to play.

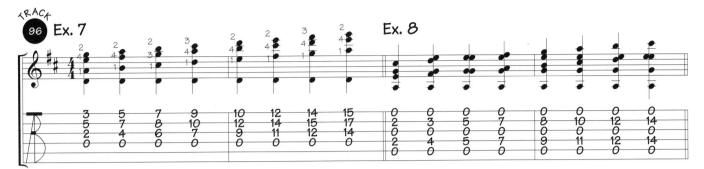

Let's continue by finding voicings based on an A7 chord. Remember that the A7 is the V chord in the key of D, so we'll be using the same scale as in the previous examples. We'll use the open A string as the bass note and construct chords on the top four strings. But since the open G and E strings are notes in the A7 chord, let's try just changing the notes on the D and B strings, to get an open-tuning sound. Moving the notes of an open-position A7 chord that fall on the D and B strings upward gives us Example 8. If we let the notes on the G string move upward with the D and B strings, we get Example 9. We're playing five-note chords here but only fretting three strings. Make sure you don't inadvertently damp the high E or low A strings.

Now let's try messing around with that voicing on the D, G, and B strings. We'll leave

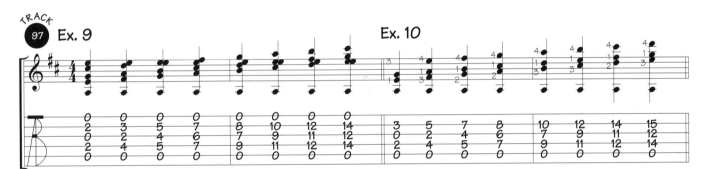

the high E string alone for the moment. As your fingers stretch to reach notes, it's a little harder to keep the open E ringing, but remember as you play this next batch of chords, that you can add the open E string anytime you want. First let's raise the higher voice a step (Example 10). Now let's also raise the lower voice a step (Example 11), giving us some more "piano chords" that require a bit of stretching. You'll need to finger the fourth and fifth voicings a little differently, switching from using your ring finger to your pinky on the bottom note of the voicing. For the next batch of chords (Example 12), we'll drop the high voicing back down a step to where it began, on the C#.

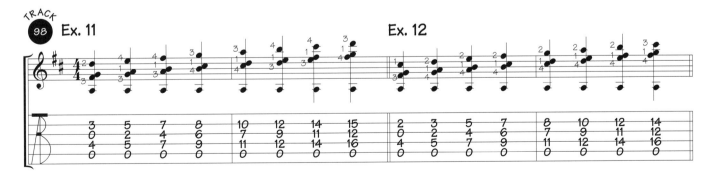

So, what are you going to do with the 88 new chords you just learned? Remember that since all these voicings are in the key of D, you can substitute them for any chord in the key of D, relying on your ear to decide what works and what doesn't. For example, try playing "Winter Waltz." The chords follow a simple D–Bm–G–A (I–vi–IV–V) progression, using voicings from Examples 3–12. Obviously, once you have to start fingering the bass notes, like G and B, your options are limited.

Winter Waltz
Music by Scott Nygaard

See if you can come up with some variations on this simple ditty, using some of the other voicings we've found. And remember that this idea will work in all other keys as well. Try moving all the voicings down two frets and adding a C note to the bottom to get some modal chords in the key of C. And if you're working with a bass player or another guitarist who's playing basic triads, you'll have even more fun, because you can experiment with modal voicings without having to worry about playing the bass notes.